HOW TO SAVE THE PLANET
ON A STUDENT BUDGET

HOW TO SAVE THE PLANET
ON A STUDENT BUDGET

KATE AYDIN

ONEWORLD

OXFORD

A Oneworld Paperback Original

Published by Oneworld Publications 2009

Copyright © Kate Aydin 2009

ISBN 978–1–85168–686–5

Typeset by Jayvee, Trivandrum, India
Cover design by James Nunn
Printed and bound in Great Britain by Bell & Bain, Glasgow

Oneworld Publications
185 Banbury Road
Oxford OX2 7AR
England
www.oneworld-publications.com

To all the people out there dedicated to saving the environment. For my husband, Ersin, who supports me in everything I do and to all the people I've worked with over the years who have been a constant source of inspiration and ideas.

CONTENTS

ACKNOWLEDGEMENTS viii

INTRODUCTION x

1 How can we make a difference? 1

2 Reducing our carbon footprint 7

3 Water 31

4 Sustainable buildings 43

5 The 3 Rs 45

6 Food and drink 73

7 Eating out 105

8 Studying 115

9 Shopping for essentials 119

10 Lookin' good 127

11 Clothes 136

12 How clean is your house? 146

13 Nature 149

14 Travel 159

15 Green-collar jobs 171

16 Fun and games 177

SHOPPING LIST 193

TEMPLATES 196

FURTHER READING 209

ACKNOWLEDGEMENTS

Thanks are due to many people who have contributed to or helped in the production of this book: Marsha Filion and Martina Adlington at Oneworld Publications for editorial support and brainstorming sessions; Hannah Shipton for her expert advice on cosmetic ingredients and the panel of student advisors who provided invaluable guidance from a student's perspective (Phil Gradwell, Andrew Hey and Alex Barker from the University of Oxford and Jacquelyn Truong (MJ) from Yale University). I'd also like to acknowledge the following organisations whose websites have been a source of valuable information: Abel & Cole, Accelerated Compost Ltd, B&Q, BCTV, Building Research Establishment, Earthwatch, Environmental Association for Universities & Colleges, Fairtrade Foundation, Furniture Reuse Network, Greenpeace, International Union of Conservation, Marine Conservation Society, Marine Stewardship Council, National Union of Students, People & Planet,

ACKNOWLEDGEMENTS

Responsible Travel, Riverford Organics, The Soil Association, Surfers Against Sewage, The Ecologist, Wiggly Wigglers and WWF. And finally a big thanks goes to all the people I've collaborated with on various environmental projects over the last eight years, who are working hard to conserve the environment for future generations.

INTRODUCTION

This book is aimed at university students, for whom the experience of living away from home in student accommodation or a shared house and taking part in university life presents not only real opportunities to be eco-friendly but also to influence housemates, lecturers and even the university. It aims to address the areas most relevant to student life, from studying, to shopping, partying and sports, and recognises that day-to-day living can be tricky when you are managing a tight budget and essay deadlines are looming.

Each section in this book has ideas for ways to reduce your impact on the environment. No matter how small your action is, it really does count because there are at least two million other students in the UK who might be doing the same thing!

LIGHT GREEN Light Green is for mega-busy students who don't have much time to do their bit for the environment but would like to do something.

DEEP GREEN Deep Green is for eco-warriors (or eco-worriers) who are already involved in environmental campaigns but want to do more.

CALL TO ACTION Call to Action gives ideas for actions you can take to encourage your university, or other organisations you want to lobby, to do more for the environment. There are some email/letter templates at the end of the book to save you time.

TOP TIPS Top Tips help you go that extra eco-mile.

Enjoy the journey …

1

HOW CAN WE MAKE A DIFFERENCE?

Every little thing we do for the environment makes a difference. Many small actions add up to one big one, especially as there are about two million university students in the UK. Turning off a light may not seem to be of huge significance in the great scheme of things but if you multiply that by two million, it can save thousands of tonnes of carbon dioxide emissions (CO_2). Student action is a powerful force for environmental change. Many student groups are pressing their universities to improve their environmental performance and these campaigns have achieved a great deal. But remember, you don't have to campaign – this book will show how you can help the environment even if you don't have time for that.

Freshers' Fairs offer a great opportunity for rallying students to environmental causes. It helps if you have lots of (environmentally-friendly!) goodies to give away: Fairtrade chocolate, recycled notepads, cotton 'bags for life' and

Fairtrade organic cotton wool pads are popular choices. Ask your Student Union (SU) for ideas on getting hold of free or cheap give-aways. Sometimes companies will donate goodies to Freshers' Fairs, as it's good publicity for them.

HOW DO I KNOW IF MY UNIVERSITY IS ECO-FRIENDLY?

Universities are huge institutions, with substantial environmental impacts (think about how much paper is used every day or how many computers are running on campuses) but the good news is that pressure from students, staff and government has contributed to a real change in universities' attitudes to the environment. Most universities now have environmental strategies and targets. Before embarking on an environmental campaign, try to find out what your university is already doing (look on the university website or contact the university Estates Department).

Environmental Association for Universities and Colleges

The Environmental Association for Universities and Colleges (EAUC) has a membership of over 260 institutions. Its website (www.eauc.org.uk) is a good source of information on what universities are doing to improve their environmental performance and is full of practical information and case studies on university environmental projects. The *Get Sorted* webpage (www.eauc.org.uk/sorted) is an online tool for universities that want to get involved with environmental initiatives. It has lots of useful information you can use as ammunition in your arguments about why your university should be doing more. *Get Sorted* also provides university staff with guidance on why saving the environment is important and what to do about it.

National Union of Students

One of the best ways to start any environmental action in your university is to visit your SU to find out what campaigns are already going on. The National Union of Students (NUS) (www.nus.org.uk) is committed to environmental and ethical change. The NUS *Sound Sourcing Guide* encourages all NUS suppliers to be environmentally-friendly and the *Carbon Academy* project aims to reduce the CO_2 emissions of the SU movement by over 5,000 tonnes per year. The NUS is involved in constructive engagement with large companies, such as Coca-Cola®, Coors® and Matalan, to encourage ethical and environmental improvements.

The NUS also runs the annual *Sound Impact* Awards (www.soundimpact.org.uk) for universities that excel in environmental improvements. Universities that have won the *Sound Impact* Award include:

- Leeds Metropolitan: diverted 95% of demolition waste from landfill on one of its building projects.
- Sheffield Hallam: set up an eco-friendly travel scheme for staff and students.

- East Anglia: built low carbon academic buildings.
- Edinburgh: since 2001, has reduced waste by 17% and increased recycling by 150%.
- Glasgow: saved over £10 million by implementing environmental sustainability improvements.

Other NUS environmental projects include an energy-efficiency research project by NUS Services Ltd to save CO_2 emissions and identify ways to reduce energy consumption in places such as bars, clubs and games rooms. In the pilot project, the NUS, suppliers and 21 student unions are studying the energy use of soft-drink machines, beer-coolers, plasma televisions, fridges and other electrical equipment. From the results of the pilot project, the NUS will develop a series of energy reduction guidance sheets for student unions. To find out if your university is involved in the scheme contact the Ethical & Environmental Committee of NUS Services (e&e@nussl.co.uk).

People & Planet

People & Planet (www.peopleandplanet.org) is the largest student network in the UK campaigning to protect the environment, defend human rights and end world poverty. There are People & Planet groups in 63 British universities and colleges. People & Planet also publish the Green League (www.peopleandplanet.org/gogreen/greenleague2008) – an environmental performance rating system for universities. In 2008, the

University of Gloucestershire was ranked first in the People & Planet Green League. It was the first English university to achieve ISO 14001 – an environmental management system that organizations can use to control and reduce their impacts on the environment. ISO 14001 overlaps into sustainability issues in the university curriculum. The University of Gloucestershire has been using energy from renewable sources since 1993 and was the first customer of *Ecotricity* (a 'green' electricity company). The university has solar-powered car park pay and display machines, recycles rainwater and uses photovoltaic cells for electricity production. It also has a sustainable procurement policy and Fairtrade accreditation is embedded in its contractual arrangements with suppliers.

Green Gown Awards

The *Green Gown* Awards are awarded to universities and colleges who have achieved innovative environmental improvements, including energy reduction, water efficiency, social responsibility and sustainable construction. The 2007–2008 award winners included:

- University of Gloucestershire (for continuous improvement)
- University of Dundee (energy and water efficiency)
- Somerset College of Arts & Technology (sustainable construction)
- London College of Fashion (social responsibility).

2

REDUCING OUR CARBON FOOTPRINT

Reducing our carbon footprint means reducing the total amount of energy produced, by saving energy through using less gas, electricity and oil. You can save energy directly (for example, turning off your computer when it's not being used) and indirectly (for example, buying locally-grown apples instead of apples that have been transported across the world).

Energy efficiency

Saving energy is good for your pocket, through lower bills in your house or university accommodation. Energy is used for just about everything – lighting, heating, cooling, transport and the manufacturing of goods we use every day.

Oil and gas are finite resources; the world's supplies are gradually running out, with no guarantee of their long-term continued availability. The challenge is to find new forms of affordable energy that won't cause pollution and climate change: solar farms in deserts, off-shore wind farms and hydro-electric power. Until the world has its energy sorted, it's really important that we use the gas and oil remaining as efficiently as possible.

Consider a simple example – the energy needed to produce a Christmas tree:

- Livestock produces manure for the tree (energy needed to raise livestock).

- Manure is transported to the forest to fertilise the tree (energy needed for transport).

- Water is abstracted from the local reservoir to water the tree for many years (water abstraction requires energy).

- Mechanised saws and transport are used to harvest the tree (power tools require energy).

- The tree is wrapped in plastic netting (plastic made from oil).

- If the tree is grown abroad, it is transported by lorry to the exporter's warehouse, shipped from the warehouse to the UK and transported to the UK warehouse (fuel for transport).

- If the tree is grown in the UK, it is transported to a warehouse and on to the shop (fuel for transport).
- A customer buys the tree and takes it home by car (fuel for transport).
- The tree is watered for a few days (water abstraction uses energy).
- The tree is taken to the local recycling centre after Christmas (fuel used for transport).
- Recycling centre takes the tree to a processor to be chipped (fuel used for transport and chipping machine).
- Chippings are taken to a company that sells chippings to garden centres (fuel for transport).
- Customers drive to the garden centre to buy chippings for their garden (fuel for transport).

You don't have to analyse everything you use to this extent but it's useful to understand the complexities of measuring and reducing CO_2 emissions.

The Climate Change Bill

The energy challenges facing your university are considerable, as the cost of energy has risen substantially in recent years. At the time of writing, the UK government's target is to reduce greenhouse gas emissions by 80% by 2050, based

on 1990 emissions levels. (Greenhouse gases are gases such as CO_2 and methane, whose increased levels in the atmosphere are generally agreed to be responsible for increasing world temperatures.)

Although many industrial companies already report their emissions under the EU Emissions Trading Scheme, your university is likely to have to report on its greenhouse gases (not just CO_2) in the near future, because in 2008 the UK government introduced the Climate Change Bill, which sets out a legal requirement for companies, including public sector organisations such as universities, to report on their greenhouses gas emissions by 2012.

RENEWABLE ENERGY

'Renewable' means energy produced from inexhaustible sources (as opposed to finite energy sources, such as oil and gas). Renewable energy includes solar energy from the sun, geothermal heat from underground, wind power, water power (hydro-electricity) and energy from crops (sometimes called 'biomass') that can be replaced quickly. However, renewable energy solutions are not without their problems: for example, growing biomass crops can damage wildlife and ecosystems, and wind and hydro-power installations can damage bird and fish habitats. As the world becomes more experienced in harnessing renewable energy, solutions will hopefully be found for these emerging problems.

Encouraging the use of renewable energy while you're at university can be tricky, because it's up to your landlord or the university to install things like solar panels, micro-wind turbines and geothermal systems, which can be expensive. Some universities already have such installations and others buy 'green electricity' which comes from wind or hydro-electric power sources.

You could consider lobbying for your university to include renewable energy in the designs for its new buildings and refurbishments and to switch to 'green' electricity. If you want to persuade your landlord to switch to renewable energy in your house, Ecotricity is an energy provider that doesn't charge extra for renewable energy. To compare energy prices, go to a comparison website such as www.uswitch.com.

CALL TO ACTION If your university has not already switched to electricity from renewable sources, write to the university Estates Department to ask them if they would consider switching to a renewable energy provider. It may cost more but it will demonstrate the university's commitment to invest in renewable energy and reduce its environmental impacts. You can see which universities already purchase green energy on the Green League website: www.peopleandplanet.org/gogreen/greenleague 2008.

Renewable energy gadgets

You can power your computer, laptop, mobile phone or iPod® with solar energy. The Freeloader Globetrotter is a device made up of small solar panels, which you leave outside or clip to your bag or rucksack. It uses solar energy to charge its batteries and can then be connected to your gadgets. To see the Freeloader, go to www.solarkitsdirect. co.uk.

Wind-up radios and torches are powered by renewable energy – human effort! They're widely available from shops such as Argos, or from online shops such as www. ethicalsuperstore.com and www.windup-products.com. By turning a hand crank, you charge them up. Most also take AA batteries and come with a mains charger in case your arms are out of action.

Solar-powered torches are ideal for festivals and camping. Many kinds are available, from waterproof torches to ones that double up as battery chargers.

REDUCING ENERGY AT HOME

Being efficient with your use of energy is a very effective way to reduce CO_2 emissions and reduce your energy bills. Quick and easy actions include turning off equipment at the socket so it's not left on standby when not in use. Televisions, DVD players, computers and phone chargers use almost as much energy on standby as when they're being used.

In the next section, I'll take you through each room in the house, highlighting where you can turn off equipment and reduce CO_2 emissions. If you share your house with others, it can be hard work getting everyone to turn electrical equipment off unless you're all of the same eco-friendly mindset. Sometimes showing people how to do things works better than telling them.

There are physical as well as psychological barriers stopping people turning equipment off. Physical barriers are easier to tackle, so start with them. Your housemates might complain, for instance, that if they turn the DVD player off, they have to re-set the clock or re-programme the player; maybe the socket is behind heavy furniture or piles of junk; perhaps several pieces of equipment are plugged into one extension lead or perhaps people don't know where the switches are or how everything is hooked up.

 TOP TIP Buy an extension lead with an indicator light. Plug electrical items (for example, television and DVD player) into the same extension lead so you can turn off all the equipment in one go. Extension leads of this type are available from most DIY shops.

Living room

- Television: televisions use a lot of energy, even when on stand-by. A colour television on stand-by uses

24% of the energy it uses when it's on, so turn it off at the socket when it's not being used.

- VCR: do you really use your video recorder or are you just keeping it for the clock? Many people prefer DVDs, BBC iPlayer or Channel 4's 4oD, so perhaps you could switch the VCR off altogether. There must be another clock somewhere!

- DVD player, radio, decks: turn them off at the socket when not in use.

- Mobile phone, iPod®, MP3 player: switch chargers off at the socket once the equipment has charged. Chargers continue to use energy even after you've detached the equipment: prove it by touching the charger ten minutes after you take your phone out – the charger will still be warm to the touch. If 18,000 students unplugged their phones once they're charged, it would save the amount of electricity needed to light 31 average houses for one year.

LIGHT GREEN Carry out a 'socket audit' in your bedroom and try to arrange the electrical equipment so you can turn everything off when you go to bed or leave the room for more than an hour.

DEEP GREEN Sit down with your housemates, draw up a basic plan of where all the electrical equipment is and decide how best to arrange everything so it can be turned off easily. You might need to think about whether extension leads are needed if sockets are too difficult to reach.

Kitchen

- Cooker: if you're only heating small amounts of food, for example soup or baked beans, don't turn the heat right up. Control the heat setting so you only heat what you're cooking and not the outside of the pan. Use the correctly-sized saucepan for the size of the plate or gas ring.

- Oven: in the winter, after you've used the oven, turn it off but leave the oven door open so the residual heat can warm the kitchen for a while (it helps if you have a clean oven of course – you don't want the house to smell of oven chips).

- Dishwasher: new dishwashers with A+ energy ratings are more energy-efficient than older models. You may have no choice over the type of dishwasher you use (if it's your landlord's or the university's property) but a fully-loaded new dishwasher is likely to use less water than washing-up and rinsing by hand. However, studies on dishwasher efficiency tend not to include the whole life cycle cost, from manufacturing the machine in the first place to the energy used to dispose of it when it's reached the end of its life.

TOP TIP If you live in a shared house or university accommodation, fill the dishwasher completely and switch it on at the end of the day, instead of everyone washing up separately several times a day. Use eco-friendly dishwasher tablets, such as Ecover.

• Washing machine: most new washing machines are energy-efficient (an AAA energy rating is the most efficient). Some have energy and water-saving features, such as measuring the exact amount of water needed per kilogram of clothes. To maximise efficiency, fill the washing machine completely but don't cram too much in. If you share a house, arrange the washing schedule so that everyone's white clothes, coloured clothes and dark clothes are washed in big batches. Most clothes (unless they're very dirty) can be washed at 30°C. However, bedclothes should be washed at 60°C, to make sure dust mites are killed. (Don't look at a magnified version of a dust mite or you'll never sleep again). If your machine has a 'short cycle' option, select it in order to reduce washing time.

- Tumble dryer: even new, energy-efficient tumble dryers use a lot of energy; hang clothes outside if the weather and your type of accommodation allow. The UK doesn't have ideal drying weather but wind will dry clothes even if the sun isn't shining. Try to use the tumble dryer as an exception rather than the norm.

- Iron: review your ironing practices. Does that sheet really need to be ironed? Will anyone notice if you don't iron your underwear? If you buy clothes that don't need ironing you'll reduce your energy bills and CO_2 emissions. Fold clothes such as T-shirts and jeans carefully when they're dry and they'll 'iron' themselves when you put them in the airing cupboard or wardrobe.

- Fridge: most new fridges are energy-efficient. If you have an old fridge, you can improve its efficiency by defrosting it as soon as ice forms in the ice tray or any part of the fridge. Don't use a de-icing liquid, because it pollutes the environment – just turn off the fridge for a few hours to melt the ice (put newspaper under the fridge door to mop up water spills as the ice melts).

TOP TIP In the winter, instead of clogging up the fridge with cans and bottles of drinks, put them in a shady area in the garden in a bucket so they are naturally chilled.

- Kettle: buy a kettle with a see-through 'window' so you can see how much water you're putting in. Boil only the amount you need. Learn how much water you need for one cup and multiply by however many cups you're making. If you have a kettle without a window, pour water into a mug first and then pour it into the kettle, so you boil exactly what you need. Using a kettle to boil hot water for cooking potatoes or pasta is more energy-efficient than putting a large pan of cold water to heat up on the hob.

Bedroom

- Computer: computers use a lot of energy. A computer running for 24 hours uses about £60 worth of electricity a year and causes 716kg of CO_2 emissions. If you leave your computer monitor on overnight, it'll consume enough energy to laser-print 800 pages. Seventy-five per cent of a computer's energy use is used by the monitor. Screensavers don't save energy, so if you don't turn off your computer when you leave the room, at least turn off the monitor.

  Set up your computer so that it automatically switches off when it hasn't been used for a few minutes. Ask your IT department or a friendly techie to help you.

LIGHT GREEN Turn off your computer, monitor and printer when you are away from your computer for an hour or more. If 18,000 students switched off their computers at lunchtime and before going home, it would save enough energy to power 5,000 low energy lights for one year.

DEEP GREEN Identify all the IT equipment in your bedroom and whether any of it is left on standby for long periods. See if you can devise a system to turn off every single piece of equipment at once.

CALL TO ACTION If your university is not already taking action to reduce computer-related energy use, write to the university Computing Department to ask whether they are developing a strategy that includes IT energy efficiency. Tell them about the Low Carbon ICT project, based at the University of Oxford, which publishes findings on computing-related energy savings. Their aim is to demonstrate how energy and cost savings can be achieved through developing technologies that reduce carbon emissions, without affecting the core strategic goals of the University. The results will be used to inspire other organisations, including universities, by providing tangible, practical examples of how to implement IT energy-saving systems that reduce costs and contribute to the overall reduction of CO_2 emissions.

- Alarm clock: an electric alarm clock uses electricity day and night, adding up to a sizable amount of CO_2 emissions if you consider the thousands of electric alarm clocks in the UK. If you have a battery-powered clock, consider using rechargeable batteries. Batteries contain toxins (such as heavy metals like cadmium) that can be harmful to the environment unless they're recycled. Battery recycling facilities are becoming more common in the UK; some universities provide them.

    Wind-up clocks use no electricity, and are more reliable, as they're not vulnerable to power cuts.

LIGHT GREEN Use a battery-powered clock with rechargeable batteries.

DEEP GREEN Use a wind-up clock.

CALL TO ACTION If your university doesn't yet recycle batteries, write to the Purchasing Department or Environment Officer to ask whether they can start battery recycling. An incentive that's worth mentioning is that it's illegal for businesses, including universities, to put batteries in the normal waste bin (batteries from offices, etc., are classed as business waste) and they should be removed by a waste contractor licensed to dispose of hazardous waste.

Bathroom

Toothbrush: dentists claim electric toothbrushes are better for your teeth, as they do the job more thoroughly, but if you brush your teeth very well using a manual toothbrush, it's just as good. It's surprising how long it takes to get rid of plaque (you can buy disclosing dye from the dentist that shows where the plaque is on your teeth – it will surprise you) so if you do switch from electric to manual to save energy, make sure you continue to clean your teeth thoroughly.

TOP TIP When you replace your toothbrush, reuse the old one for cleaning hard-to-reach muddy areas on your bike or for general household scrubbing in small places.

- Hairdryer: do you really need to use a hairdryer? Unless it's very cold and you don't want to go out with wet hair or you need to have perfect hair because you're going to a glamorous event, don't spend ages drying your hair – just wash and go.

- Shaver: some people prefer electric shavers, especially if your style is designer stubble or complicated beardy patterns. If you just need a straightforward shave, use a non-disposable refillable manual razor.

- Baths and showers: it's nice to have a long, relaxing soak at the end of the day but in the morning it's quicker and more energy-saving to shower. If you have one bath to every five showers you'll save energy and cut your energy and water bills. Baths don't need to be completely full, especially in summer when the weather's hot; you won't get too cold if you fill it half-full and have a splash around.

LIGHT GREEN Limit baths to one per every five showers.

DEEP GREEN Have one bath per twenty showers (or one bath per month).

Lighting

- Reduce your carbon footprint and reduce energy bills by switching off lights when you're not using them and using low-energy bulbs.

- When studying for long periods, use an Anglepoise® lamp fitted with a low-energy bulb to give you concentrated light and enable you to turn off the other lights in the room.

- Turning lights off in shared spaces like landings and halls can be tricky, as you don't want to accidentally plunge your housemates into darkness. Remind your housemates to turn lights off by sticking 'switch it off' labels under the switches.

- Low-energy bulbs (sometimes called Compact Fluorescent Lightbulbs – CFLs) last up to ten times longer

23

than standard (tungsten filament) bulbs. In the past, low-energy bulbs gave out less light than standard bulbs but new ones are just as bright. Another type of low-energy bulb are LEDs (light-emitting diodes); these are more expensive than CFL bulbs but last for 60,000 hours.

Visit the Eco Street website (www.eco-st.co.uk) to calculate how much energy you could save if you swapped standard light bulbs for low-energy bulbs.

WATTAGE CONVERSION TABLE

Ordinary Light Bulb	Energy-saving Bulb	Watts Saved
100W	20W	80W
60W	11W	49W
40W	9W	31W
25W	5W	20W

- Low-energy bulbs contain mercury, so they should not be put in the normal waste bin. Your university should already have a system for recycling low-energy bulbs; if not, contact your Health and Safety Officer for information on the legal requirements for bulb disposal, and/or discuss with your Environment Officer. If you live off the campus, contact your local council to find out if they offer low-energy bulb recycling services.

LIGHT GREEN Fit your room with low-energy bulbs if you are responsible for changing your own light bulbs.

DEEP GREEN Ask your housemates to start a kitty to collect money to gradually replace standard bulbs with low-energy bulbs in the whole house.

TOP TIP Before you rush off to buy low-energy light bulbs, make a note of the fitting (bayonet or screw-fit) and the maximum wattage – it could save a wasted trip!

CALL TO ACTION Write to your university Estates Department to ask what the plans are for reducing the energy emissions from lighting. Ideally, your university should have an energy strategy outlining plans to reduce CO_2 emissions that includes details of energy-efficient lighting.

• Technology is changing quickly; hopefully your university Estates Department is actively researching the most energy-efficient lighting for new buildings and refurbishments. They may even be able to put you in contact with someone in the department who can give you useful information on the best low-energy bulbs to use. You could then take this information back to your Environment Committee/ faculty or SU to use in other university-wide energy campaigns.

- Ideally, low-energy bulbs should have the Energy Saving Trust blue label, which shows they have rigorously tested and approved the design.

- Candles: candles give a lovely, gentle ambient light but you may not be able to burn candles if you live in student accommodation, as they can be a fire hazard. However, not using candles has other benefits: they produce smoke which can be breathed in. The US has banned lead wicks in candles but the UK has not yet followed suit. Unfortunately, there is no legal requirement for candles to be labelled with a full list of ingredients, so it can be hard to know what's in them. It is possible to buy natural candles (that don't contain petrochemicals) from specialist websites but they are very expensive. To create atmosphere, use a lamp with a dim low-energy light bulb.

CALL TO ACTION Write to your local supermarket and/or home furnishing shop to ask whether they plan to phase out toxic ingredients in their candles and put a full list of ingredients on their candle packaging.

- Natural lighting: daylight stimulates the brain to produce natural 'feel-good' endorphins, so take advantage of natural light and reduce your energy consumption at the same time. Keep windows clean and your curtains or blinds fully open during the day to let the daylight in. If your room is dark (and if you're allowed to paint it), consider painting it a light colour and use light-coloured furnishings, bedding and rugs. These will reflect light around the room and make it appear brighter.

LIGHT GREEN If your room or house has dirty windows, give them a good wash and keep the curtains fully open during the day (tie the curtains back to keep them open if necessary).

DEEP GREEN If you live in, and have heavy curtains or blinds that don't open properly or very dirty windows that you can't manage to clean yourself, ask your university or landlord if they can arrange to get them cleaned.

- Vending machines: vending machines generate money for universities, because vending machine companies pay to have them sited in corridors and bars. Vending machines use about £400-worth of electricity a year if left on continuously. If switched off overnight and at weekends, the CO_2 emissions from the vending machine's energy use would be reduced by 1 tonne per year.

LIGHT GREEN Buy your own drinks/crisps/chocolate from a shop instead of using a vending machine. You'll save money, too.

 DEEP GREEN Instead of buying bottled water from a vending machine, take your own water bottle with you (or flask of tea/coffee).

 CALL TO ACTION Ask your university whether they can turn vending machines off at weekends and overnight or if they'd consider getting rid of them altogether. You may need to present a business case considering, for example, the energy costs saved per year compared to the profit gained by the university by housing the vending machine.

 TOP TIP Some vending machine suppliers provide Fairtrade products in their machines. Your university may be interested in contacting a Fairtrade vending machine supplier. One of the suppliers used by universities is Selecta UK Ltd (+44 [0]121 748 9620).

FEEL THE HEAT

It's astonishing that in the twenty-first century, in one of the richest countries in the world, many British people still live in poorly-insulated houses! We spend the winters shivering and lamenting the cold and can need the heating on any time between September and June (ten months!).

Insulation

When looking for a place to rent (and I appreciate you may not have the luxury of shopping around to find the perfect accommodation), inspect basic levels of insulation before you sign the contract. Check for obvious gaps around front doors and windows that don't shut completely. Cold air coming in means more of your money going out on higher energy bills.

If the house needs insulating but your university or land-lord won't do it, consider taking some temporary, not too expensive, insulating measures yourself using products widely available in DIY shops:

- Put draft excluder around doors or windows.
- Place special foil backing behind radiators, to reflect heat back into the room.
- Lag your boiler and pipes.
- Lay thick rugs or mats, to stop drafts coming up from under the floor.
- Hang thick and heavy curtains at the windows – and draw them when it gets dark.

Be cool

Living or studying somewhere that gets very hot in summer, and has poor ventilation, is not much fun. Air-conditioning is not common in the UK, which is a probably a good thing because the energy it uses is responsible for considerable CO_2 emissions, but it can be desirable when temperatures soar above 30°C! You might live in a building where the heating and cooling is not under your control. If it is too hot and you can't turn the heat down, apart from the obvious measures such as opening windows, there is little you can do. Swap your duvet for a sheet at night and keep curtains or blinds closed during the day to stop the sun heating up the room.

If your house or place of study does have air-conditioning, control it by:

- Setting the room temperature no lower than 22°C
- Setting the controller so the room is only cooled if someone's in it (or if research equipment needs to be kept cool)
- Closing doors and windows to avoid cooling the outside world
- Putting blinds on windows to keep out the sun
- Checking that the heating is off when the air conditioning is on
- Opening windows first thing in the morning to 'pre-cool' the space
- Making sure the air con is working at maximum efficiency – ask the university Estates Department how often the cooling system, fans, filters, etc., are checked (they should be serviced annually).

3

WATER

UK drinking water is among the cleanest in the world but water companies are under pressure both to meet the increasing water demands of a growing population and to ensure that polluting chemicals, such as nitrates and pesticides, don't build up in the water supply. The extra costs of maintaining high-quality water are the reason why our water bills are expected to rocket in the future.

WHY SAVE WATER IF IT RAINS ALL THE TIME?

Water availability is as crucial to global security as climate change and food security. Many experts think that water could be second only to oil as the cause of international conflict. Globally, the availability of freshwater is steadily decreasing – a trend that is expected to continue as the world population expands towards the nine billion mark and drought conditions due to climate change get worse. The increasing water demands of growing

economies, the effects of climate change and contamination caused by severe flooding are mounting problems.

You might think the UK has more than its fair share of water but actually the south-east is as dry as some Mediterranean countries. According to the Environment Agency, the south of the UK has less water available per capita than dry areas of Spain and Portugal – which is hard to believe after the seemingly constant rain and flooding the UK experienced in 2007 and 2008!

British water companies want to invest billions in water improvements between 2010 and 2015, to ensure long-term guarantees for water quality and supply and flood protection. This means average water bills will rise by about £30 each year. Nearly all the water companies are increasing prices at levels above the inflation rate; according to the water regulator, OFWAT, water bills have increased by 42% in real terms since 1989 (when the water industry was privatised).

It's easy both to reduce the amount of water we use each day and to help improve water quality. 'Quick wins' include having showers instead of baths, being careful about what we put down the plughole and into the drains and using eco-friendly bath products and detergents.

HOW CAN I CUT MY WATER BILLS?

If your house is fitted with a water meter, you'll only pay for the water your household uses. If you don't have a meter, you'll be charged a relatively high rate, based on the water consumption of an 'average' family that runs several washing machine loads each week, washes the car every Sunday, has lots of baths and waters the garden with a hosepipe. If you share a house with, say, three other people, you could save money by getting a water meter fitted, but you need to ask your landlord's permission first. Water authorities fit meters for free.

Do you live in a water scarcity area?

Water scarcity in the UK? Surely not! But Folkestone and Dover Water has officially designated the area it covers as a Water Scarcity Area. This means that the company can install water meters in people's homes without needing a request from the homeowner. To be granted water scarcity status, the water company must convince the government that there is a significant, long-term deficiency in water supplies. The question is, will more areas in the UK be designated Water Scarcity Areas in the future? To find out which water company you come under, look at the OFWAT website (www.ofwat.gov.uk).

KEEP IT CLEAN

There's more to water than simply getting enough of it. The population of the UK is growing (from 61 million in 2008, it is expected to increase by 2.8 million by 2016) – and more people equals more chemicals and other unsavoury items being flushed down toilets and down plugholes and drains.

The UK's drinking water is very good quality but there is evidence that, even though water goes through extensive purification treatments, traces of anti-cancer drugs (such as bleomycin) and psychotropic drugs (such as the sedative, diazepam) are starting to be seen in our water supplies. These pharmaceuticals mainly enter water through effluent. Although the levels of these chemicals are currently well below safety levels, according to the Drinking Water Inspectorate, they need to be monitored very carefully. The water companies are working to develop mechanisms to prevent these substances building up, but use of these drugs is increasing and filtering processes cost money, resources and energy.

Individually, we may not be able to do much about anti-cancer drugs getting into the water but we can reduce other types of pollution such as by using eco-friendly surfactants in detergents, soaps and household cleaning products. You can find eco-friendly products both in High Street shops and online – see the Shopping List at the end of this book. Body products such as soap, shower gel, shampoo, conditioner, shaving lotion and toothpaste can contain nasty chemicals; if we cut down on their use, less will get into our sewers.

Hundreds of chemicals pollute our environment – albeit under official safety limits – some of which are classified as 'persistent', meaning they don't break down and therefore build up in the environment. Some scientists are beginning to believe that certain chemicals, increasingly found in sea- and fresh-water, can cause liver damage, cancer and neurological diseases. These chemicals include endocrine disruptors (substances such as pesticides, fungicides, insecticides, oral contraceptives and industrial chemicals), which disrupt the production of hormones in the body. Evidence shows that residues of oral contraceptives that are discharged into the sewer system can find their way back into our drinking water. One of the results of this could be the decreased sperm count in men, while in marine animals, hormone pollution can lead to birth abnormalities, damage to the immune system and growth and breathing difficulties.

LIGHT GREEN Each time you stock up on shampoo, shower gel, conditioner, or any soapy bubbly stuff, make sure it's eco-friendly.

DEEP GREEN Write to your university to ask what it's doing to minimise chemical pollution beyond the legal limits required by the Environment Agency. Ideally, the university should have a documented waste strategy or water strategy, which addresses pollution.

REDUCING WATER USE

Most people think they don't use all that much water. It's just a little stream of water coming out of a little tap – and it disappears so quickly. But when you add up the quantities of water we use in a day, the figures are quite astounding. On average, every day, every person in the UK uses 140 litres of water. Here are some suggestions on how you can reduce your water consumption.

Bathroom

An average bath uses 80 litres, while a five-minute shower uses about 35 litres (although power showers can use 70 litres), so by having a shower instead of a bath you'll save about 45 litres of water. If two million students had a shower instead of a bath that's 90,000,000 litres saved each time!

Used bath water (when you do have a bath) is known as 'grey water'. Grey water doesn't look particularly attractive but you can use it to water garden plants (if you've used eco-friendly cleansing products). It can be messy carrying water down the stairs, through the house and into the garden, so if you can afford it, Wiggly Wigglers (www.wigglywigglers. co.uk) sells bath water siphons online for around £20. Siphons suck the water out of the bath down a tube and on to the garden through the window (easiest if your bathroom overlooks the garden). A garden hose uses 500 litres per hour, so you'll save lots of water watering the garden this way.

Toilet

Old toilets have large cisterns and use about six litres of water or more per flush. Modern toilets, with smaller cisterns, can use as little as 4.5 litres of water per flush. Putting a brick in the cistern reduces the volume, thereby using less water each time you flush. If you put a brick in your cistern, be very careful it doesn't interfere with the ballcock or any other part of the flushing mechanism.

> **TOP TIP** Put the plug in the sink when you wash your face, instead of washing under a running tap. This saves about six litres of water for each minute spent washing.
>
> Turn the tap off when you brush your teeth and save 12 litres of water in an average two-minute tooth-brushing session.

Kitchen

An average washing-up bowl holds about five litres of water. Depending on how many changes of water you use, you could end up using 20 litres of water each time you wash up. A modern dishwasher uses about 15 litres per cycle, so if stacked full, uses less water than washing up by hand.

If you have a dripping tap in your house or hall of residence, arrange to get it mended as soon as possible. Even a slightly dripping tap can waste 140 litres a week. You might be tempted to try to do the job yourself but if you're living in rented or university accommodation it should be done by your landlord or university. Mending a tap requires specialist tools and if you end up causing damage or flooding, you might have to pay for repairs.

If your washing machine is less than ten years old, it will use about 50 litres per cycle but if it's older than that, it could use as much as 100 litres. Washing machines are usually provided by your landlord or the university so there's not much you can do if you are stuck with an old, inefficient one, except to ask them to buy a new replacement. If they agree, ask them to get a very energy-efficient model (AAA rating). Most new machines have a 'short wash' option for clothes that are not very dirty, which also saves water. If you don't know what the programmes are on your washing machine because the manual has gone walk-about, you can download manuals from the Internet (www.washerhelp. co.uk). You'll need to know the make and model of your machine.

Wash vegetables in a bowl instead of under a running tap and you'll save about 20 litres of water each time. If you have a garden, pour the dirty water on the plants.

Garden

With your landlord's permission, set up a water butt to collect rainwater, which you can then use to water the garden.

Make sure the butt is installed correctly – most of the major DIY store websites have advice on setting up water butts.

WATER MILES

You've heard of food miles (the number of miles food is transported from the field to the supermarket shelf) – now there are water miles! 'Water miles' refers to the amount of water used to grow a product before it's exported. Some people call this concept 'water footprint', by analogy with carbon footprint.

The water footprint of a 250ml glass of beer is 75 litres – mostly used to produce the barley – which is nearly as much water as an average bath. We usually don't think how much water a bunch of flowers, an apple or some meat has used before it gets to the shops but there's a growing concern about how much water is being used in developing countries to grow food for the developed world. Many countries in the developing world are experiencing prolonged drought, due to climate change and, for example, to water supplies being allocated for growing flowers for sale in UK supermarkets. In these countries, many people don't have enough water for themselves or their livestock.

Shrink your water footprint by buying seasonal produce, grown in the UK or Europe. Tropical fruit, vegetables, flowers and meat grown on the other side of the world have a larger water footprint than locally-grown products. You can calculate how large your water footprint is on the Water Footprint website (www.waterfootprint.org).

LIGHT GREEN Reduce your water footprint when you shop – buy at least two items of seasonal fruit or vegetables grown in the UK or, as a second-best, in Europe.

DEEP GREEN Only buy seasonal British fruit and vegetables (for example, only buy strawberries in summer).

4

SUSTAINABLE BUILDINGS

You may not be able actively to do much about sustainable buildings unless you're studying to be an architect or engineer – in which case you are an important agent for change in the future of sustainable building design. Most universities have substantial building and refurbishment programmes, with significant environmental impacts, because they use large amounts of natural resources (building materials, energy and water). Development produces waste and can destroy the green spaces that are wildlife habitats. Once built, buildings continue to be a source of greenhouse gas emissions and waste for many years.

The Building Research Establishment (BRE) has developed an environmental assessment method for assessing new buildings and refurbishments in the higher education sector. The method provides guidance for reducing the environmental impact of a building and contains guidance on high-quality building insulation, reducing greenhouse gas emissions, increasing water efficiency, reducing waste, improving indoor air quality, enhancing biodiversity through landscape design and using sustainably-sourced materials, such as FSC timber (FSC timber is grown in responsibly-managed forests and doesn't contribute to rainforest destruction). The BRE is also developing sustainable laboratory design guidelines for university buildings.

The EAUC has produced two detailed guidance documents on how to achieve high-performance buildings, which cover issues such as adaptability, smart layouts, modular structures, natural lighting and ventilation, healthy user environments, low energy and water consumption, limited carbon footprint and the use of renewable, non-toxic and recycled materials. The reports demonstrate the business benefits of sustainable buildings, including lower energy, water and maintenance costs, reduced risk of unaffordable rises in energy bills, reduction in inflexible buildings that are difficult to adapt to changing requirements, better employees' health and improved performance and reputation.

If you are thinking of campaigning for your university to build sustainable buildings, it's a good idea to familiarise yourself with the information on the EAUC website so you can clearly communicate to your university the type of sustainability criteria to which you want the buildings to adhere.

5

THE 3 RS

Reduce, Reuse, Recycle.

We all produce waste, even those of us who try really hard to create as little as possible. Reducing waste at source is the best way to deal with it. As landfill sites fill up, and raw materials become increasingly scarce, we need to re-think the way we dispose of materials. Reusing waste is the second-best option; for example, reusing glass jars to store dried herbs or pasta. Recycling is third-best: while it's commendable to recycle, re-processing waste materials into new products still uses energy and natural resources and creates CO_2 emissions.

THE TRUE COST OF WASTE

The true cost of waste is the money it costs to dispose of something, plus the cost of making it in the first place. Throwing something like a plastic bottle away is estimated to cost five times more than the simple cost of waste

disposal, once the cost of the materials used to manufacture and transport the bottle is taken into account. This is significant for cash-strapped universities, which can save significant amounts of money by aiming for zero waste and thinking carefully about the disposal of the items they buy.

In the UK, the government's Landfill Tax is rising; the cost of sending waste to landfill is increasing by about £8 per tonne each year. This has led some organisations to reconsider the amount of waste they send there. In the future, companies will design their products to reduce waste to a minimum and built-in obsolescence (for example, washing machines designed to last no longer than ten years) will probably be a thing of the past. An interesting development is that landfill sites are already starting to be excavated by waste companies, which see a business opportunity in recycling the valuable resources that lie beneath. Waste experts say it's only a matter of time before our landfill sites are dug up to get at the resources they hide.

Until a time in the bright future when there is no waste (when everything will be reused, recycled or used to generate energy), some waste is going to be created as a result of day-to-day living.

Zero waste

How can we reduce waste at source? Achieving zero waste is almost impossible in today's throw-away culture but we can do a lot to reduce it to the bare minimum.

First, we need to get a grip on the way we feel about waste. Waste isn't very glamorous and understandably, most people aren't hugely interested in it. We point the finger at other people: why don't supermarkets cut down on packaging? Why doesn't the government set up furniture reuse schemes everywhere? Why doesn't my university compost food waste? While we wait for 'them' to find solutions for better waste management, we can take our own steps towards zero waste.

How much waste do you produce? As an experiment, write down every bit of waste you produce in one day, including at university – it might surprise you. Once you know what sort of waste you produce, you'll be able to find solutions to reduce it.

How to reduce waste

If you don't have access to recycling facilities for certain types of waste, here's how you can reduce, reuse or recycle it:

- Plastic corks: only buy wine with natural cork stoppers (real corks can be composted or used as fire lighters).
- Clingfilm: use storage containers to keep food in the fridge instead.
- Supermarket packaging: buy loose fruit and vegetables (don't be intimidated when your apples roll

down the conveyor belt at the till and the shop assistant gives you a withering look).

- Plastic rings from six-packs: buy loose beer cans instead (the rings can harm wildlife if they get into the environment, and they take hundreds of years to break down).

Don't know how to reuse unwanted items?

- CDs – if the university has an allotment, hang CDs on sticks near the plants to keep birds away or use them as coasters for hot drinks.
- Broken crockery – instead of throwing broken mugs or plates in the bin, crunch them up into tiny bits by stepping on them with sturdy shoes (think of your favourite enemy!) and mix them into the garden soil to improve drainage, or use as drainage in plant pots.
- Plastic bags – use bags to cover your bike saddle to stop it getting wet in the rain (and use a cloth bag for shopping from now on).
- Old medicines/prescription drugs – take these to any pharmacy and they'll dispose of them safely.
- Clothes, books, shoes – take to recycling banks (large supermarkets often have them in the car park or go to your local council waste recycling centre) or hold a Swap Shop (see page 141).

- Printer paper – use the blank side of print outs for taking notes instead of buying notepads.

- Water filters (for example, Brita) – can be recycled in some High Street shops such as Argos, Robert Dyas, Cargo, Sainsbury's, Homebase, Asda and Makro, but ask at the shop first.

- Old glass jars – use to store dried food, rice and pasta.

Most universities and local authorities provide recycling facilities for paper, cardboard, plastic (for example, plastic bottles and food packaging), glass, tins, aluminium (for example, take-away cartons and baking foil) and cans. Some waste can't be recycled because it's made from mixed materials, for example plastic crisp packets with metal coating on the inside (with the exception of 'Jonathan Crisps', whose bags are made from recyclable plastic). Some recycling facilities don't yet exist in the UK; for example, cork recycling.

To find out more about recycling possibilities in universities, have a look at Waste Aware Campus (www.wasteawarecampus.org.uk), a new Scottish initiative with information and ideas on how students can set up waste reduction and re-use schemes in universities.

If you set up a snazzy recycling system in your house or university accommodation, don't spend too much time cleaning cans, bottles and other recyclable items. They don't need to be spotless: a quick rinse with cold water usually does the trick – or soak them in the water left after you've washed up. It's counter-productive to use lots of washing-up liquid and hot water: the aim of recycling is to use less energy and water and fewer chemicals.

If your university or council is super eco-friendly it might recycle:

- Food waste (either composting on-site or by sending it to a composting facility)
- Batteries
- Aerosols
- Low-energy light bulbs
- Printer and toner cartridges
- Cooking oil
- Unused hazardous detergents (for example, bleach)
- Household paint.

Bulky items

Some councils offer free bulky items collections, for example unwanted furniture, bikes and carpets. The items are either donated to furniture reuse schemes, recycled or sent to landfill. If you live in university accommodation, the university is responsible for making arrangements to dispose of your waste and may be able to help you get rid of any unwanted bulky items. Some cities and towns have furniture recycling projects that collect good-quality reusable furniture and pass it on to people on low wages. The Furniture Reuse Network website (www.frn.org.uk) has information on how you can donate to furniture projects near you. You could make some money by selling your unwanted items on eBay (www.ebay.co.uk) but make sure it's in good condition. Freecycle (www.freecycle.org) is a free-membership website where you can pass on – not sell – unwanted, good-quality items to other members.

PAPER, NEWSPAPERS AND JUNK MAIL

Forty-two per cent of the world's industrial wood harvest is used to make paper. This level of consumption cannot continue indefinitely, because half of the world's forests have already been destroyed and 80% of what's left is seriously degraded. Unfortunately, not all paper comes from sustainably-managed forests – much of it comes from illegally-harvested timber (from forests with fragile ecosystems). The UK is the world's second biggest importer of illegal timber!

Reducing and reusing paper is an efficient way to contribute to conserving forests and reduce consumption of natural resources. The next best option is to buy paper with recycled content and/or FSC certification. Saving the rainforests will also help to slow down global warming, as they store 50% of the world's carbon. Deforestation accounts for 15–20% of the world's total CO_2 emissions. As trees are cut down, carbon is released which contributes to global warming and climate change.

Making recycled paper uses many fewer trees and much less oil than virgin paper, so save the rainforests and only buy recycled and/or FSC paper, notepads and any other stationery products. According to the Environment Agency, manufacturing one tonne of recycled paper uses 64% less energy and 50% less water and causes 74% less air pollution than making the same quantity of virgin paper. For every tonne of recycled paper we use instead of virgin paper, we save 15 trees, 2½ barrels of oil, 4,132 kWH electricity (enough to heat a home for six months), 31,319 gallons of water and 29 kg of air pollutants. Paper accounts for about a third of landfill waste, where it produces methane, a greenhouse gas that is 23 times more potent than CO_2.

Printer and photocopier paper

Printing and photocopying in universities uses tonnes of paper. On average, each person in the UK generates 100 pieces of paper a day, which end up as waste. Ideally, paper recycling should be standard by now in every university and council kerbside collection. If your university is not yet recycling paper, ask the Purchasing Department or Environment Officer what their plans are to reduce paper waste.

Watch out for wasting paper when you print emails (hopefully you won't be printing many anyway). An auto signature can make an email run on to a second page. If you must print emails, select only the page you want to print.

IT Managers can be very helpful in finding solutions for using paper more efficiently. You may not solve all the issues at once but even simply setting printers to default to double-sided printing can immediately halve paper waste (and paper costs). (Of course, your university may insist on essays being printed only on one side of the paper, which of course you must do.) Old printers may not be designed to print double-sided; if the university has an IT Committee, ask them if they plan to buy printers that will minimise waste of paper. Alternatively, contact the Environment Officer in your university to push the issue on your behalf.

 LIGHT GREEN Buy recycled and/or FSC paper.

 DEEP GREEN Re-use unwanted printer paper for taking notes and only buy stationery, such as notepads and card file dividers, made from recycled and/or FSC content.

 TOP TIP Re-use old newspaper to mop up large water spills, clean windows and wrap up broken glass. Store newspapers where everyone can find them in an emergency.

CALL TO ACTION If your university doesn't yet buy recycled/FSC paper and other stationery, contact the university Purchasing Department and/or Environment Officer (or ask the SU to contact them on your behalf) to ask what their procurement strategy is for recycled paper and other recycled products.

E-zines

There are so many ways to get our news these days – you may not be a fan of newspapers but if you do buy a paper, after you've read it, fold it tidily and put it where someone else might read it or give it to another student. Reading the news on the Internet cuts down on paper, although the experience of reading the paper in bed with a cup of tea on Sunday mornings is still preferred by many. E-zines are an alternative to newspapers and many are free. Some contain useful information on environmental issues and eco-ideas. Get informed and win pub arguments! Some great examples include:

The Ecologist (www.theecologist.org), which contains the latest updates, with high-quality images, on environmental issues that affect us all, from GM crops to overfishing, to what's in some of the products we use every day.

People & Planet (www.peopleandplanet.net) is a must for students and provides you with the latest news on student environmental initiatives and information on where your university ranks in the UK's 'Green League' for universities.

Tree Hugger (www.treehugger.com) covers a wide number of interesting environmental topics, providing news, top tips and good photos.

Stop junk mail

Companies put tonnes of junk mail – over £25 billion worth each year – through our doors and most of it is neither read nor wanted. Producing junk mail uses a lot of energy, water and chemicals. Don't let junk mail find its way into your house – put a 'NO FREE NEWSPAPERS OR ADVERTISING' sign on your front door. You can also sign up to the Mailing Preference Service (www.mpsonline.org.uk), which removes your name and address from companies' mailing lists. It is supported by the Royal Mail and the Information Commissioner's Office. If you sign up to receive 'updates' on a company's latest products, you're signing up to junk mail; don't do it unless you really want to know. Make it very clear you don't want their junk; you might have to search for a teeny-weeny tick-box in the small print.

Cardboard

It should be possible to recycle cardboard boxes and packaging either in your kerbside box or at your university.

Cardboard is good for composting if you have a compost bin; tear the cardboard into pieces of roughly A5 size (if you leave cardboard outside when it rains it's much easier to tear up).

Paper cups

Universities produce quite a lot of paper (and plastic) cup waste. If your university canteen only provides disposable cups for drinks, reduce waste by getting your own thermos flask so you can have a hot drink whenever you want.

Universities are big organisations, with considerable purchasing power. Waste reduction requirements should be included in all tender documentation for catering contracts. Contact your university Purchasing Department or Environment Officer to ask what plans are in place for including waste reduction in the overall procurement strategy. If your university insists on using paper cups, they should at least be made from recycled and/or FSC paper.

Toilet paper

Twenty-five million trees are needed each year to produce the UK's toilet paper: on average, each person uses around 100 rolls a year. If everyone in the UK switched to recycled toilet paper, we could make huge environmental improvements.

LIGHT GREEN Buy recycled toilet paper (it's sold in most supermarkets).

DEEP GREEN Buy recycled kitchen towels (if you use them).

 CALL TO ACTION If your university doesn't buy recycled toilet paper or paper towels, contact the Purchasing Department (or ask the SU to contact them on your behalf) to ask whether the university is considering switching to using recycled toilet paper and paper towels and including this in the tender documentation for cleaning contracts.

PERSONAL HYGIENE WASTE

If personal hygiene waste, such as cotton buds, tampons and condoms, is flushed down toilets, it can eventually be washed into the sea, polluting beaches and seas and causing damage or death to wildlife; for example, condoms can be mistaken by marine animals, such as turtles, dolphins, fish and birds, for food; if they eat them, the animals can suffer a slow, painful death. Always put condoms, cotton buds, tampons and other sanitary products in the bin (cotton buds made wholly from cardboard can be composted).

 LIGHT GREEN Buy cotton buds made from cardboard-based material instead of plastic.

 DEEP GREEN Sign up to Beachwatch (www.adoptabeach.org.uk) and volunteer to clean a beach for one day a year (or go with a group of friends from university).

LIGHT GREEN Most universities and councils recycle glass bottles and jars, or you can take them to a bottle bank. Old large glass jars make good storage containers for rice, herbs, pasta, sugar, salt and tea bags. Clean the jars and dry thoroughly before re-using.

TOP TIP Get a sturdy box to store your empty glass bottles and jars, ready for recycling in your kerbside collection or bottle bank. This will keep them out of the way and they won't clutter the kitchen.

PLASTIC BAGS

If you have old plastic bags scrunched up in a corner in the kitchen, make sure they're readily to hand, so you can grab one before you head off to the shops. Re-use plastic bags until your collection runs out and then get a cloth 'bag for life' so you don't accumulate any more. Bags for life are available in most supermarkets and shops or your council may give them out for free (contact your council to find out). Cloth bags are better than jute or very thick canvas bags, because they easily fit into your pocket, rucksack or bag.

Manufacturing plastic bags uses energy, water and oil and produces waste. Although the idea of reusing plastic bags and using cloth bags is slowly catching on the UK, each year supermarkets give out an average of about 290 bags per person. Of these 17½ billion plastic bags, 80 million get blown into parks, rivers and on to beaches. 10,000 animals including whales, turtles, birds and other livestock are killed by swallowing plastic bags each year.

If every British student refused plastic bags at the check-out, we'd save about 600 million bags a year!

 LIGHT GREEN Re-use plastic bags by carrying one or two in your bag or pocket at all times (you never know when you might get the urge to shop).

 DEEP GREEN Refuse all plastic bags in shops and use a bag for life instead. These can be made of reinforced plastic, canvas, cotton or jute. The best general-purpose type of bag is made of cotton. String bags are excellent for supermarket or clothes shopping – it's amazing how much stuff you can fit into them.

CALL TO ACTION Write to your local supermarket to ask when it will stop handing out all plastic bags to customers. If French supermarkets can manage to do it, why can't ours?

 TOP TIP Wrap gifts in a new bag for life instead of wrapping paper – you never know, it might inspire the recipient of the gift to switch to using one.

FOOD WASTE

Sixty per cent of the waste in your bin is likely to be food and other biodegradable waste. According to WRAP (Waste and Resources Action Programme), in the UK, we throw away 6.7 million tonnes of food a year. That's around ten billion pounds' worth of food that should have been eaten – enough to fill Wembley Stadium eight times.

Although food waste is biodegradable, when it is in a landfill site it can't rot down completely, because as it gets packed down by other rubbish dumped on top of it, air is pushed out of the landfill and the bacteria that break down the waste are starved of oxygen. As a result, the food putrefies (turns into a dark, smelly liquid). Putrefaction also produces methane, a greenhouse gas 23 times more potent than CO_2.

To prevent unnecessary food waste, work out a rough idea of what you're going to eat during the week, so you only buy what you need and avoid throwing away uneaten food. For example, salad can go off quite quickly, so instead, buy green vegetables, such as courgettes or broccoli, which last for longer in the fridge.

Don't worry too much about the sell-by date on food; most food is fine to eat at least for a short time after that date, although you should be careful with meat, eggs and fish. Don't automatically throw food away because the label says so – use your common sense to decide whether it's edible or not. If it smells horrible or looks weird, don't eat it.

Composting

The most eco-friendly way to get rid of food waste is to set up a compost bin in your garden or back yard (if you have one). Not only will this reduce the contents of your rubbish bin by 60%, it will prevent methane emissions. Compost is a free, non-chemical fertiliser for your garden, although you won't get huge amounts. A standard-sized compost bin (330 litres) will produce about two sacks' worth of compost a year.

Look on your council website to see if it sells discounted compost bins. The Recycle Now (www.recyclenow.com) website sells discounted compost bins and has lots of information on how to set up and manage your compost bin. Most compost bins are made from plastic and look like Daleks with a lid. They are very light and easy to install, as long as you have a small patch of earth in your garden or yard. You can buy compost bins from garden centres but they may cost more than the council's.

SETTING UP YOUR COMPOST BIN

- Site the bin somewhere in the garden that you can get to easily: you won't want to trudge halfway down the garden on a wet Sunday morning. Choose a sunny place if possible, because heat helps the bacteria break the food down quickly.

- Dig a circle about 5cm deep and just a little wider than the diameter of the compost bin. Put the compost bin over the circle to make sure it fits. Place the bin in the circle and shovel the earth you've just dug back into the compost bin until it's about 10cm deep, making sure there are no gaps around the bottom of the bin, to keep small animals from crawling in. As an extra precaution against animal squatters, you can place a large-ish square of chicken wire (from a DIY shop) underneath the bin (before you put the bin in place), extending beyond the diameter of the bin so animals can't crawl in from underneath. I myself have never used chicken wire and have never found squatters in my compost but it's up to you.

- Create a 'base' to ensure your compost 'works' properly. Make a layer of torn cardboard, twigs and newspaper at the bottom of the bin, to about 10cm deep. This will allow air to circulate at the bottom of the bin. Then add a 10cm layer of vegetable peelings or garden waste, such as old leaves.

- After a few days, you can add just about anything you want to your bin. Food waste – including dairy products and small bits of meat – is fine but don't put large bones in, because they'll never break down and so have to go in the waste bin. The lid on the compost bin will stop any smells from getting out and in any case, a properly-working compost bin shouldn't smell offensive.

Some people keep wormeries instead of creating a compost bin, if they don't have a garden. The worms eat your food waste and turn it into compost. Wormeries can be kept on a patio or in a cool place inside the house. But the worms can escape – so be warned! Wormeries are fairly high-maintenance; worms don't like certain types of food (for example, citrus peel) or extreme temperatures and the wormery has to be drained regularly to remove waste fluid. (You can use the fluid to fertilise garden plants.) Worms need looking after – if you go on holiday and leave them they'll probably die from drowning in their own waste fluid. You also have to buy worm nutrient products every so often to supplement their diet. For a student household, where people are likely to go away for holidays or at the end of term, a wormery might be a bit too time-consuming. If you have a garden, it's far better to have a compost bin.

SURPRISING THINGS YOU CAN COMPOST

You can compost quite a few things as well as food and garden waste: the vacuum cleaner's contents (lint and dust), cotton buds (only ones made of cardboard), cotton wool, paper towels and tissues, hair (birds like this to make nests with, so you could hang it on a branch in the garden instead), toilet roll tubes and cotton tampons.

COMPOSTING IN UNIVERSITIES

The University of Aberystwyth is embracing a new method of composting, which does not smell or attract vermin and is very easy to use. It's called 'in-vessel composting' and uses the 'Rocket Composter' produced by Accelerated Compost Ltd (www.quickcompost.co.uk) to turn food waste into compost very quickly. This system is especially useful for catering food waste.

The Rocket is a continual process, fed daily with food waste from kitchens and wood chippings from the university's parks and gardens. Equal quantities of food and chippings are put into the hopper. The process is automated: the blades of the Rocket Composter's internal shaft turn to aerate the food waste and wood chippings, moving it along the body of the machine, creating loading space at the input end of the machine and pushing finished material from the output end. It takes about two weeks for compost to be made. The Rocket is a controlled environment, in which harmless composting bacteria thrive. In its warm, moist, well-ventilated and food-rich environment, they eat, multiply their numbers and break down the food waste. This generates heat, which keeps the environment warm and the bacteria working. A Rocket Composter costs a few thousand pounds but will last for years, so it's a worthwhile long-term financial investment (you save money from reduced rubbish collections and get free compost for the university grounds).

LIGHT GREEN If you live in private accommodation with a garden, contact your local council to find out if they sell cheap compost bins (if you live in a university residence, ask the Environment Officer what's involved in setting up a compost bin).

DEEP GREEN If you already have a compost bin, start adding more items from the list above, such as used paper towels and cotton wool.

TOP TIP Carry a small sealable container in your bag to hold biodegradable waste such as apple cores, banana skins, tissues and paper towels. Take it home and put it in the compost at the end of the day.

CALL TO ACTION Contact your SU to see whether they would help to campaign for an in-vessel composter to be installed in the university, to recycle the university's food waste. You can get technical information from www.quickcompost.co.uk.

PIZZAS, BURGERS AND TAKE-AWAYS

Take-away food packaging can include paper bags, boxes, plastic trays, polystyrene bases, aluminium cartons, waxed paper packaging, plastic bags or cling film. Cardboard and aluminium trays and pizza boxes can be recycled, unless they're very dirty (rinse aluminium trays in the water that you've used to do the washing up). It might be possible to recycle plastic take-away containers in your kerbside box or university recycling (but usually polystyrene and cling film can't be recycled).

LIGHT GREEN Limit your take-aways to two a week.

DEEP GREEN If your local take-away uses excessive or non-recyclable packaging, write to them asking them to consider switching to recyclable packaging.

TOP TIP If ordering from home, cook your own rice to go with your take-away, to reduce packaging waste and save money.

ELECTRONIC WASTE

Increased consumption of electronic goods has led to a growing problem of electronic waste, especially in developing countries. The United Nations estimates that the world's electronic waste is expected to be above 40 million tonnes in the near future. The European Environment Agency has calculated that the volume of electronic waste is rising three times more quickly than any other type of household waste.

Electronic waste is often shipped to developing countries for dismantling and re-processing, countries where environmental protection and health and safety laws are often ignored. Electronic waste causes pollution to local communities; many people working with electronic waste become ill or die from heavy metal poisoning. Electronic waste contains poisons such as lead, arsenic, antimony trioxide, poly-brominated flame retardants, selenium, cadmium, chromium, cobalt and mercury. If disposed of irresponsibly, these toxic substances can seep into soil and groundwater, harming the local environment and people's health.

In 2007, the United Nations launched a global initiative to reduce the global mountain of electronic waste. This includes setting standards for extending the life of electronic goods and improving the market for second-hand equipment. Dell, Microsoft, Ericsson and HP have all signed up to the scheme.

Your university should have clear guidelines for electronic waste disposal. If you are not aware of the guidelines, ask the university Environment Officer or Health & Safety Department where you can find them. If you live outside the university, you'll most likely have to take electronic waste to the council's recycling centre, which will have containers for depositing old computers, laptops, keyboards, etc. Check your council website for information.

Some electronic companies will remove your old equipment when you buy new equipment from them –

commonly known as a 'take-back' scheme. If you're planning on buying new electronic equipment, ask the company
beforehand if it provides a take-back service.

Printer cartridges

Your university may already recycle used printer and pho-
tocopier toner cartridges; it's a very easy thing to do. Some
cartridge-recycling companies raise cash for charity by selling the cartridges to processors who dismantle the cartridges and recycle the components. If your university
decides to sign up to such a scheme, it's important that the
company can demonstrate the electronic waste is not being
shipped to developing countries for processing, as this
increases transport-related CO_2 emissions and the dismantling process often causes environmental pollution in
developing countries.

If you want to persuade your university to recycle toner
cartridges it might help to provide the Purchasing
Department with a list of some of the companies that other
universities use for cartridge recycling, such as:

- Lyreco – www.lyreco.co.uk
- Supplies Team – www.supplies-team.co.uk
- Office Green – www.officegreen.co.uk
- Greensource Solutions – www.greensource.co.uk

- The Recycling Factory – www.therecyclingfactory. co.uk
- Environmental Business Products – www.inkagain. co.uk
- Recycle Cartridge – www.recyclecartridge.org.uk

LIGHT GREEN When your printer cartridge runs out, take it to the university to be recycled if it has cartridge recycling facilities.

DEEP GREEN If your university hasn't yet set up cartridge recycling facilities, contact the university Environment Officer to ask how cartridge recycling facilities could be installed in the university (it might be useful to send them the list of cartridge recycling companies above).

Mobile phones

Mobiles contain toxic heavy metals and should never be chucked in the bin. They can be easily recycled, either through mobile phone shops when you buy a new handset or through a charity, such as Vodafone's *fonebank* service (www.fonebank.com or 0207 404 6440). Fonebank accepts most working mobile phones and provides a free collection for organisations with more than 15 working mobiles to recycle. It will track how many phones are recycled and the amount of cash raised or donated to charity as a result. The National Trust recycles mobile phones, through Office Green (information@officegreen.co.uk or 0800 502050), and offers free collections for ten or more mobile phones.

6

FOOD AND DRINK

In 1962, in her book *Silent Spring,* Rachel Carson pointed out the dangers of using certain chemicals in farming; chemicals which can build up in the environment and enter our food chain. To create a future where food and drink are not contaminated with chemicals, we need to increase the use of, and improve, environmentally-friendly farming methods. There may be some disadvantages to organic farming – for example, it can lead to lower yields – but many people still feel that's preferable to having to ingest chemicals.

As well as increasing concern about the range of chemicals we are consuming, the argument over organic and genetically-modified crops continues to rage. No one knows for sure what the long-term impact of GM crops on living things and the environment will be. And as if GM worries are not enough, global warming is causing extreme drought and flooding in many countries, leading to crop destruction, food shortages and famine.

Recent outbreaks of diseases like bluetongue (which affects cows and sheep), bird flu and swine fever are matters of great concern. Pollination is in decline due to drastic decreases in bee populations, especially in the USA and Europe. Scientists don't know for sure why bees are in decline but they think it could be partly caused by destruction of their natural habitat, climate change and disease. Reduction in pollination and climate change are leading to lower food yields and rising food costs. Some people think these problems can be solved by new technology and chemicals; others think it's best to go back to holistic methods, such as organic farming, and improve wildlife habitats.

The manufacture of pesticides and fertilisers used in food and drink production generates high levels of CO_2 emissions. Chemicals used in farming can reduce the natural bulk and fertility of soil, leading to soil erosion and rendering the area useless for growing food. It can take years to regenerate soil to be fit for growing food crops. Scientific studies on pesticide and fertiliser contamination are increasingly warning of the health problems when such chemicals get into our water supply and food, linking them to cancer and other diseases of the immune system.

Much of our food is transported to the UK from across the world; as well as contributing to global warming, these cheap meats, fruits and vegetables are often from countries with low levels of environmental responsibility and animal welfare. Fish stocks around the world are in serious decline and many species are on the verge of extinction. Sometimes, you'd question whether humans really are an intelligent species!

SUPPORT SUSTAINABLE AGRICULTURE

Purchasing power is a powerful mechanism for change. Ten years ago, a complete smoking ban was unthinkable and the notion that supermarkets would sell only Fairtrade bananas (Sainsbury's is planning to phase out non-Fairtrade bananas) and free-range eggs would have been considered radical. As consumers, we can support sustainable agri-businesses by buying food and drink that is produced according to sustainable principles – protecting the environment, the economy and society from negative environmental impacts and helping to ensure adequate supplies for future generations.

The challenges of the twenty-first century, such as food shortages, population increase, energy security and climate change are very likely to alter the way we produce our food and may bring about an entirely new model. Agricultural practices will have to evolve, to cope with climate change, water pollution, increasing population, species extinction, disease, energy availability and the depletion of natural resources.

FUN AT THE SUPERMARKET

Should I buy organic food if it's transported from countries on the other side of the world? Should I buy local food if it's not organic? Should I buy organic packaged food or non-organic non-packaged food? Free-range or woodland eggs? Organic wine or Fairtrade wine?

You can be excused if you come to a complete halt and let your eyes glaze over when you attempt to shop in an eco-conscious way: the jury is still out on many of these issues. If you live near a farm shop or a shop selling local produce, it's better to patronise it than a supermarket, as you'll be supporting local producers. However, most universities are in cities or suburbs, so the supermarket may be your only option.

Knowing for sure what's best for the environment requires a detailed analysis to see how much CO_2 was emitted in the production and transport of each product, how much water, natural resources and chemicals were used to grow it, what the farmer's profits were and, if appropriate, what were the animals' welfare conditions. The issues are complex and most people don't have time to weigh up all the pros and cons when they're shopping for food or drink, but you could consider:

- Have synthetic chemicals been used to grow it? – non-organic food is likely to contain synthetic chemicals so buy organic.

- Is it made from animals/animal products from depleted stocks? – to avoid eating fish from depleted stocks, switch to a sustainably-sourced brand (look for the Marine Stewardship Council label, for example).

- Is it from animals that have been intensively farmed? – for foods such as eggs and meat, switch to a free-range version.

- Has it travelled very far to get to the supermarket shelves? – buy seasonal food grown in the UK instead.

- Has it been produced using large amounts of water in countries suffering drought? – again, buy seasonal food grown in the UK.

- Is it heavily packaged? – a lot of organic food is pre-packed, to stop it getting mixed up with the non-organic produce. However, supermarkets are increasingly using biodegradable corn starch or vegetable-starch packaging, which can be composted if you have access to a compost bin.

IS ORGANIC BETTER?

Would you like some chemicals with that, sir and miss?

Imagine if, instead of a giant pepper grinder, the waiter brought you a little bottle with a skull and crossbones on it.

Would you drizzle its contents over your food? Many of the synthetic chemicals sprayed on non-organic produce come in containers labelled with 'poison' symbols, because they're toxic. One way to avoid toxins is to opt for organic food and drink.

Is organic food better for us? You'd think that this would be a straightforward conclusion – after all, who wants to eat chemicals? There isn't any conclusive evidence that organic food is better for you, although some studies show that rats fed on organic food are healthier than non-organic rats. If it's good for rats, maybe it's good for us! While the jury is still out on the merits of organic food, you can make a decision based on whether you think it's a good idea to ingest chemicals and opt for organic food and drink if you don't.

Our health isn't the only issue. Organic farming has other benefits, such as improving soil conditions by using natural fertiliser and creating chemical-free wildlife habitats that encourage pollinating insects and other wildlife to breed. Organic farming doesn't use nasty chemicals that can leak through the soil into the groundwater (where much of our drinking water comes from) or into the sea and on into fish – and so into our fish and chips.

Organic food can cost more; as a student on a tight budget, you don't have to buy everything organic. Even if you buy just one organic item next time you go shopping, you'll at least make a difference to the environment, because other people will be doing the same thing all over the country.

IS GM FOOD A PROBLEM?

Is genetically-modified food dangerous to humans, animals and the environment? Scientific arguments from both the pro-GM and anti-GM lobby appear to be equally convincing. Very few of us are scientists working in the field or have read every single academic paper on GM. With a lack of conclusive evidence, how can we accurately weigh up the pros and cons? Some people feel that certain questions have not been answered (and backed by independent scientific evidence) adequately by the biotech companies:

- Are GM ingredients safe to eat?
- Is it safe to produce GM vaccines and other drugs in the same crops we use for food and animal feed?
- Can we control GM contamination or will we lose the choice of non-GM food and crops?
- What effect will GM have on our wildlife and environment?
- Does GM really produce higher crop yields?

In 2005, a poll was carried out to assess UK citizens' opinions of genetic modification. Eighty-seven per cent said they did not want to eat GM food. Regardless of this, the government is still supporting GM crop trials in the UK.

To assess the pros and cons of GM, the findings and opinions of 400 scientists were commissioned in the *International Assessment of Agricultural Knowledge, Science and Technology for Development* report. Their conclusion was that 'assessment of GM technology lags behind its development, information is anecdotal and contradictory and uncertainty about possible benefits and damage unavoidable'. If 400 scientists from around the world agree that there is considerable uncertainty about GM technology, perhaps we should be just a little bit concerned that our government's intentions are to embrace GM technology, allowing GM crop trials to be conducted where contamination can occur.

Up until February 2007, there had been 216 recorded incidents of GM contamination of non-GM crops around the world. GM contamination is largely irreversible. If GM crops contaminate organic farms, they can no longer be certified organic, so organic farmers cannot stay in business. If GM contamination continues, eventually we'll have literally no choice but to eat GM-contaminated food (even though, ultimately, it might not be safe for us or the environment).

Some people are pro-GM because they believe that the technology can produce enough food for everyone in the world and prevent famine in developing countries. Although it would be brilliant to find a techno-solution to world hunger, there is no evidence that GM is it. Billions of pounds have been spent on the development of GM crops but there is no evidence that they have higher yields than non-GM crops. This means that they may not 'feed the world' as the biotech industry said they would. According to the *International Assessment*, we don't need technology such as GM to prevent global hunger; we just need to reduce our consumption in the developed world and develop fairer systems of distributing food and wealth. Examples of unbalanced wealth distribution are the replacement of food crops by crops grown to make plant-based oil (biodiesel) and the heavy agricultural subsidies of wealthy nations. Food crop decline leads to starvation and malnutrition in many parts of the world – and these could be changed by human action alone.

How can I get my university to switch to non-GM food?

You will find it useful to prepare beforehand, so that you can articulate your argument as clearly as possible. Instead of browsing the web late into the night for relevant information, it might be quicker to contact organisations, such as the Soil Association (www.soilassociation.org), that have already consolidated many of the peer-reviewed papers on GM crops. As part of your campaign you could write to the relevant departments in your university (for example, Purchasing or Catering) to enquire about the university's policy on non-GM food and drink. Ask to see the university sustainable procurement policy, and details of the implementation plan and targets. You could also ask whether the university's tender documents include criteria for non-GM food and drink for catering contracts. Ask your SU to campaign for sustainable procurement in the university on your behalf if you prefer. Ask the university Environment Committee to add GM issues to the meeting agenda (they may ask you for more information about this, so be prepared) or ask the university catering managers what the plans are to ensure GM food is not used in the university.

LIGHT GREEN Buy organic milk, as a large number of GM crops are made into animal feed which is fed to animals used for non-organic meat and dairy products.

DEEP GREEN Buy organic dairy products, vegetables and fruit (and organic meat if you're a meat eater).

CALL TO ACTION Join up to the non-GM campaign! The GM Freeze website (www.gmfreeze.org) has lots of information on how you can campaign to stop GM.

TOP TIP Look for the Soil Association symbol on food and drink so you can be sure the food or drink is organic and adheres to the Soil Association's high standards.

If you want the choice not to eat GM products in the food you buy, write to your local supermarket's Head Office and ask them what they are doing to ensure GM food does not end up in their products and what their timelines are for doing this (see the GM template letter at the back of the book).

- Aldi: Managing Director UK and Ireland, Holly Lane, Atherstone, Warwickshire CV9 2SQ
- ASDA: Chief Executive, Asda House, South Bank, Great Wilson Street, Leeds LS11 5AD
- Budgens: Chief Executive Officer, Musgrove House, Widewater Place, Moohall Road, Harefield, Middlesex UB9 6NS
- The Co-op: Chief Executive Food Retail, The Co-operative Group, New Century House, Manchester M60 6NS
- Iceland: Chief Executive, Second Avenue, Deeside Industrial Park, Deeside, Flintshire CH5 2NW
- Lidl: UK Director, 19 Worple Road, London SW19 4JS
- Marks and Spencer: Chief Executive, Waterside House, 35 North Wharf Road, London W2 1NW
- Morrison's: Chief Executive Officer, Hilmore House, Gain Lane, Bradford BD3 7DL
- Netto: UK Managing Director, Elmsall Way, South Elmsall, Pontefract WF9 2XX

- Sainsbury's: Chief Executive, 33 Holborn, London EC1N 2HT
- Tesco: Chief Executive, New Tesco House, Delamare Road, Cheshunt, Hertfordshire EN8 9SL
- Waitrose: Managing Director, Waitrose Central Offices, Southern Industrial Area, Bracknell, Berkshire RG12 8YA.

LOCAL FOOD

'Local' food is grown in the village, town, county or region from which you buy it. If you find it hard to buy local food, then food grown in the UK is the next best. Local food results in reduced CO_2 emissions, because it isn't shipped from the other side of the world. It also boosts the UK farming economy. However, there is an argument that certain foods grown in the UK produce more CO_2 than the same foods grown in more natural conditions: out-of-season crops grown in the UK use more artificial lighting and heating in a cold, wet climate than the same crop grown somewhere naturally warm and sunny overseas. The best way to avoid UK food that might have a large carbon footprint is to eat seasonally: strawberries in summer, apples in autumn. Look at the label on the food packaging to see if it was grown in the UK.

Grow your own

Growing your own food is as local as it gets. You may not have a garden or access to an allotment but you can grow fresh herbs and 'bushy' tomatoes in containers on a windowsill, balcony or in the back yard.

Mustard and cress for sandwiches or salads is easily grown from seed on a sunny windowsill and is a good source of vitamin C. If you can't get to a garden centre to buy seeds, get potted herbs from the supermarket. A potted basil will grow happily indoors on a sunny windowsill (only water it when the leaves are wilted, as too much water causes the roots to rot). Pick off leaves to mix with pasta or add to sandwiches.

If you're lucky enough to have a garden, dedicate a part of it to herbs. Herbs need soil with good drainage (mix small stones or bits of broken crockery into it). Thyme, rosemary and mint can be planted outdoors in a sunny area or left in their pots, as long as you don't let them dry out. Thyme and rosemary are good in pasta or meat dishes. Mint is great for salads or mixed with boiled potatoes.

Tomato plants are easy to grow if you water and fertilise them properly. You can even grow them on a patio, using a 'grow bag' in a sunny position. If you grow tomatoes, make sure you're going to be around to water them in summer. You might need to use organic fertiliser, which you can buy in most garden or DIY shops.

Start an allotment

Allotments – havens of peace and chirping birds; hazy days relaxing in a deckchair watching the clouds go by … not quite. There's a lot of work to be done on an allotment before you can stand back and admire!

Why are allotments important? They provide opportunities to meet other like-minded people, get some fresh air and physical exercise and, of course, low-cost fruit and vegetables. On a wider scale, allotments are excellent training grounds for acquiring the skills needed to obtain your food in the future. Food policy analysts are pressing the government to plan a strategy for ensuring the UK population has continued access to food staples in a time of energy shortages and climate change. Fossil fuel is a key component of the fertilisers and pesticides used in food production and, of course, is used to transport food around the world. At present, the UK imports more than 90% of its fruit but in future, due to rising oil prices, it probably won't be feasible to import apples from the USA or New Zealand.

According to analysts, the UK needs to revolutionise its food industry, by planting orchards on a massive scale, moving livestock production to hill farming to cut down on grain fed to animals, and getting the UK population to eat less meat and dairy produce. We need a self-sustaining, eco-friendly way to grow our food. One way to do this is to return to former farming methods, re-learn gardening skills, change our diet and stop feeding livestock so much grain and let them graze naturally in the hills. Currently 40% of grain grown in the UK is fed to animals, which is a very inefficient way to farm. Some universities are starting to set up allotments where students can grow their own food. Contact your SU or Estates Department to ask them to investigate whether there is a small plot of unused land on the university site where you could set up an allotment.

An allotment in a university needs to be well-organised and supported by the university management. Allotments can be high-maintenance and require start-up funds. It can cost about £10,000 to start up a properly-organised allotment scheme, with security lighting, fencing and sheds for tools and other essentials and about £2,000 a year to run. If you're operating more on a shoestring, beg, borrow and (well, perhaps not steal) tools, compost bins and seeds from local wildlife or allotment groups or perhaps try to raise funds in the university. Some cities and towns have allotments you can rent for a few pounds a year. Contact your local authority for infomation.

UNIVERSITY ALLOTMENT SCHEMES

The University of Gloucestershire has set up an allotment on an area of formerly derelict scrubland, about the size of a football pitch. The university got things going by clearing and preparing the ground. So far, 50 students have joined the scheme and their first winter harvest included onions, garlic, parsnips, potatoes and curly kale. The university reckons a student can save up to 25% on their weekly food bill of about £25 – an annual saving of around £325. The students like the allotment scheme because as well as saving them money, they get exercise in the fresh air and a chance to chat with other students while they're working.

The University of Aberdeen has a vegetable garden on campus, managed by students. The produce is used at a Fairtrade café run by the Shared Planet Society and the students also run a vegetable-box scheme.

The University of Staffordshire set up a community organic garden in April 2007. The garden operates across five allotment sites just outside the university boundaries and grows fruit, vegetables and flowers. They're working with some Chinese students to investigate which of the oriental greens can be grown successfully. The aim is to encourage staff and students to work together growing organic produce for their own use. There's no financial cost to the volunteers – they just give time and commitment. Staff and students benefit from the work both physically and mentally (the therapeutic effects of gardening can be better than anti-depressants!). The allotment has a 15m poly-tunnel and greenhouses, and soon will have a pond and wildlife garden to attract frogs and other natural forms of pest control. The organisers are considering the possibility of installing solar panels and wind turbines. The fencing and compost heaps were made from old pallets. Local people and some university staff and students bring garden waste to the allotment to compost (the allotment gate is left open to allow this) and staff who keep horses donate horse manure. They hold special shredding events, like recycling Christmas trees into woodchip for making paths.

The University of Nottingham has an allotment space for students to grow vegetables. The students asked the Estates Department if they could use some land for growing food. They agreed and ploughed the plot for the students, to give them a head start. They also gave them a water butt and set up a water supply. The students organised an allotment society which others joined. Everything that's grown is for students' consumption. Students grow potatoes, spinach, carrots, lettuce, onions, leeks and much more.

Seasonal food

Seasonal food is grown in environmental conditions that are similar to its natural environment, so it doesn't need copious amounts of water or artificial heating, which saves natural resources and reduces CO_2 emissions. Typically, seasonal food is better-quality and healthier (if it's organic). The British Food Fortnight website (www.britishfoodfort-night.co.uk) has information on how to get seasonal food cheaply and a three-minute film explaining why it's best to buy British.

SEASONAL FOOD

January	cabbage, cauliflower, celeriac, forced rhubarb, leeks, parsnips, shallots, squash, turnip
February	cabbage, cauliflower, celeriac, chard, chicory, forced rhubarb, kohlrabi, leeks, parsnips, spinach, swede, turnip
March	beetroot, broccoli, cabbage, cauliflower, leeks, mint, mooli, parsley, radishes, rhubarb, sorrel
April	broccoli, cabbage, cauliflower, morel mushrooms, wild garlic, radishes, rhubarb, carrots, kale, watercress, spinach, rosemary flowers
May	asparagus, broad beans, broccoli, cabbage, cauliflower, gooseberries, mint, new carrots, parsley, rhubarb, samphire
June	asparagus, broad beans, carrots, cherries, courgettes, elder-flowers, gooseberries, lettuce, peas, peppers, redcurrants, rhubarb, strawberries, tayberries, tomatoes
July	asparagus, aubergines, cabbage, carrots, cauliflower, celery, cherries, fennel, French beans, gooseberries, lettuce, loganberries, mange-tout, nectarines, new potatoes, oyster mushrooms, peaches, peas, radishes, raspberries, rhubarb, sage, spinach, strawberries, tomatoes, watercress
August	apples, aubergines, basil, carrots, cauliflower, courgettes, French beans, gooseberries, greengages, lettuce, loganber-ries, nectarines, peaches, pears, peas, peppers, raspberries, rhubarb, strawberries, sweetcorn, tomatoes

September	apples, aubergines, blackberries, cabbage, carrots, cauliflower, cucumber, damsons, elderberries, figs, French beans, grapes, kale, lettuce, melons, mushrooms, nectarines, onions, parsnips, peaches, pears, peas, peppers, potatoes, pumpkin, raspberries, rhubarb, spinach, sweetcorn, tomatoes
October	apples, aubergines, beetroot, cabbage, carrots, cauliflower, courgettes, grapes, lettuce, marrow, mushrooms, parsnips, potatoes, squash, tomatoes, watercress
November	beetroot, cabbage, cauliflower, chestnuts, cranberries, leeks, parsnips, pears, potatoes, pumpkin, quinces, swede
December	beetroot, cabbage, cauliflower, celeriac, celery, parsnips, pears, pumpkin, red cabbage, sprouts, swede, turnips

LIGHT GREEN Buy at least one item of seasonal food when you do your shopping.

DARK GREEN Instead of buying salads and fruit imported from abroad in winter, buy seasonal fruit and vegetables (see months November–May in the above seasonal calendar).

Order your food online

Order your food online (no, not just pizza). Online organic box companies such as Abel & Cole (www.abelandcole.co.uk)

and Riverford Organics (www.riverford.co.uk) deliver boxes of local fruit, vegetables, soups, cheese, meat, fish and Fairtrade produce to your door. The food can cost more than at the supermarket but the produce lasts a long time because it's fresh. Many people buying organic boxes notice that they spend less, compared to what they spend at the supermarket, because they don't impulse-buy so much.

The perfect eco-lunch

Take-aways almost inevitably end in a mound of packaging waste. A packed lunch is a green (and healthy) way to eat when you're out and about. Pack your lunch in a reusable container (hard plastic is very practical), instead of buying expensive, packaged sandwiches. You could include an organic apple, a Fairtrade banana and wholesome sandwiches of egg and cress, cheese or tomato. Keep a plate, knife, fork and spoon in a drawer at university (if you have one to call your own) to avoid using paper plates and plastic cutlery.

FAIRTRADE

Sainsbury's plans to sell only Fairtrade bananas in all its stores in the near future. You can get Fairtrade products pretty much everywhere now. The UK market for Fairtrade products is doubling in value every two years; in 2007 it reached an estimated retail value of £493 million. The Fairtrade Foundation has licensed over 3,000 certified products for sale through retail and catering outlets in the UK. The UK is one of the world's leading Fairtrade markets, with more products and more awareness than anywhere else. Around 20% of roast and ground coffee and 20% of bananas sold in the UK are now Fairtrade.

In 2003, there were two Fairtrade universities in the UK. Now there are over 70 – and many more are working towards getting Fairtrade status. Students and staff want the choice of having Fairtrade tea, coffee and other products. Fairtrade status is a visible sign that a university is forward-looking and actively embedding sustainability principles in its day-to-day business.

To get Fairtrade status, universities need to fulfil Fairtrade's 5 goals:

- Fairtrade foods are made available for sale in all university shops.
- Fairtrade foods are used in all cafés, restaurants and dining halls in the university.
- Fairtrade foods (for example, tea, sugar, coffee) are served at all meetings hosted by the university or college and the SU (or equivalent) and are served in all university, college and SU management offices.
- There is a commitment to campaign for increased Fairtrade consumption on campus.
- A Fairtrade Steering Group is established.

For more information on university Fairtrade campaigns go to www.fairtrade.org.uk.

By purchasing Fairtrade products, a university can help support farmers in developing countries, whose low incomes may mean they cannot afford education, clothes or even food for their children. Farmers that sign up to Fairtrade are guaranteed a minimum wage, part of which must be used on community improvements, like building schools, repairing roads and bridges and developing clean water systems. Fairtrade also encourages farmers to use fewer chemicals on their products and to switch to organic farming.

As well as supporting producers in developing countries there are other reasons why universities should aim for Fairtrade status. Pressure from the EU and UK governments and non-governmental organisations (NGOs) for universities to become sustainable has led university funding bodies, such as the Higher Education Funding Council for England (HEFCE), to include sustainability criteria in their Estates Management Statistics (EMS) reports. These reports are usually compiled by a university's Estates Department and sent to HEFCE each year. They include details of the university's energy and water use, waste and recycling levels and other sustainability criteria, such as whether the university has Fairtrade status or an Environmental Management System. The environmental data in the EMS reports are used by People and Planet (a non-governmental organisation) to collate information on all the UK universities' environmental performance for the 'Green League' which is published in the *Times Higher Education Supplement* (THES) every year. Needless to say, this proves to be embarrassing for universities at the bottom of the Green League table. Universities are awarded three points in the Green League if they have Fairtrade status.

MEAT

You may be vegan or vegetarian because of concerns about animal welfare, the chemicals used in meat production, the inefficiency of feeding large quantities of grain to animals or the slaughtering process. It's probably true that killing an animal would be difficult for many people – how many of us could kill a chicken, sheep, cow or pig? – but for some, humans eating animals is the natural order of the food chain.

Let's assume that the carnivores among you are not ready to give up sinking your teeth into roast lamb or a sizzling bacon sandwich but let's also assume you want to eat animals that have been looked after humanely. Free-range organic meat that is produced locally is likely to have been reared humanely and to contain very low levels of chemicals. Ideally, if you buy meat regularly, contact the company to ask for details of the distances the animals are transported to be slaughtered. Some organic animals are carried long distances to be slaughtered (well over three hours) and then returned to their farm to be sold as 'local' food, so check before you buy. The transport of live animals is a particularly worrying issue in the global farming industry, especially concerning the transmission of diseases that can explode into pandemics, such as bird flu or foot and mouth.

 LIGHT GREEN If you buy meat, try to buy organic free-range meat (as it's more expensive, eat meat a bit less often).

 DEEP GREEN Forgo the meat dishes when you eat out (for example, kebabs and burgers) because it's unlikely you'll ever know the origin of the meat or what's in it (unless you eat in a super-sustainable restaurant or pub, where information on the meat's origin is readily available).

FISH

The Marine Stewardship Council (MSC) recommends that consumers try to make environmentally-sustainable choices when buying fish and shellfish. An MSC label indicates the fish is from sustainably-managed stocks. You should avoid fish and shellfish from depleted stocks in favour of those from healthy well-managed ones, caught using selective methods or farmed to high sustainability standards. The

FishOnline website (www.fishonline.org) provides guidance on which fish are OK or not to eat. The *Good Fish Guide* is a pocket-sized information booklet that lists fish from sustainable sources. The guide is updated by the Marine Conservation Society (MCS) twice a year to reflect the latest situation.

According to the World Bank and the United Nations Food and Agricultural Organisation, about $50 billion is lost each year as a result of fish stocks declining. Poor management and overfishing is responsible for more than $2 trillion of avoidable economic losses since the 1970s. Global fisheries are in crisis so we need to use our purchasing power to halt the decline in fish stocks, which are shrinking because of pollution, climate change, habitat loss and unnecessary by-catch (fish caught accidentally which are thrown back into the sea). Governments are starting to take some action to help fish stocks survive, by cutting back on fleet size and reducing fuel subsidies for ships. The UK government's Marine Bill is a recent piece of legislation that hopefully will stop fish stocks declining further but the situation requires immediate action both by governments and individuals.

Quite a few supermarkets and some restaurants sell MSC-certified fish. Universities are starting to include sustainable fish criteria in their catering policies and contracts, due to student and staff pressure and as a result of developing sustainable purchasing policies and biodiversity policies. If you want to campaign for your university to only use sustainably-sourced fish, the Marine Conservation Society's (MCS) website (www.fishonline. org) is a good place to start gathering the information you will need.

Good fish

A selection of sustainably-sourced fish, taken from the MCS recommended list of 2008/2009:

albacore tuna

Alaskan pollock

Alaskan salmon

bib/pouting

black bream

cockles

coley/saithe

Cornish sardines

dab

flounder

grey or red gurnard

lemon sole

line-caught mackerel

mussels

oysters

pollack

organically farmed prawns

red mullet

organically farmed salmon

line-caught bass

spider crab

tilapia

organically farmed trout

Bad fish

The Marine Conservation Society believes stocks of these fish are the most endangered due to over-fishing or fishing methods that damage the environment and kill other non-target species. On the FishOnline website (www.fishonline.org), there is a full list of all the endangered species and you can click on each species to find out why it's endangered.

The MSC website is a great source for fishy recipes using sustainably-caught fish from healthy stocks. Even the university chefs might be interested in some of these!

If you're bored, it's raining or you have to babysit, play the fishy game on the Fish & Kids website (www.fishand-kids.org) and learn something about sustainable fishing at the same time. Children will find Murdock the fisherman's cat very entertaining. The website has some interesting fishy facts, too.

 LIGHT GREEN When you shop or eat out, take your Good Fish Guide with you, so you can be sure you choose non-endangered fish. If in doubt about where your fish is from, choose a non-fish dish.

 DEEP GREEN Only eat fish whose packaging carries the MSC logo.

 CALL TO ACTION Give copies of the Good Fish Guide to your friends and send some to the university Purchasing Department, asking them to include sustainably-caught fish in the catering contracts for the university (remind them that the Guide is updated twice a year online).

MILK, CHEESE AND EGGS

Dairy products and eggs are linked to several issues of animal welfare and sustainable farming. Factory-farmed (intensively-farmed) cows produce more milk than organic cows but the price for higher milk yields is that the factory cows have to be confined indoors for most of the year and during that time are not allowed to munch on grass or move around much. Factory-farming uses more chemicals than organic farming and factory cows are sometimes fed genetically-modified animal feed.

One argument in favour of factory farming is that in a world of increasing consumption and growing human population, organic cows don't produce enough milk to satisfy the growing demand for milk, cheese and meat, compared to intensively-farmed cows. This problem could be solved – to a large extent – if we simply consumed a bit less meat and dairy.

You can find organic cheese and milk in supermarkets, some of which is produced in the UK. However, even though farmers are diversifying by switching to organic farming, many are under severe financial pressure, because current prices for milk don't cover their costs and as supermarkets push the price of milk down further, they can't earn an adequate living. This is bad for the environment; as farmers lose money on dairy production, they have less money to invest in environmental improvements on their farms. Support the UK farming community and cows by buying organic milk (especially local organic milk, if you can find it – you might be able to get it from health food shops).

You can get organic regionally-produced milk, meat and fish from organic box schemes such as Abel & Cole or Riverford Organics. Organic box companies typically have high standards of animal welfare. For example, for animals used in Abel & Cole products the maximum journey from farm to slaughter is one hour, although most journeys are much shorter. Cattle travel no more than 25 miles, chickens travel an average of 12 miles and pigs travel eight miles. Many of Abel & Cole's suppliers have abattoirs very close to the farms where the animals are reared and 50% of the lambs are slaughtered on the farm. Abel & Cole adheres to the Soil Association guidelines for organic animal produce, which state that animals have to be healthy, rested and clean before they embark on their journey to the abattoir.

If you've ever seen Hugh and Jamie's chicken programmes on television you'll know about the horrors of battery-farmed chickens. To discourage battery farming, the solution is simple – only buy free-range 'woodland' eggs (available in most supermarkets). Woodland eggs come from chickens that live in an environment as near as possible to their natural one, with trees to roost in and lots of ground to peck. Marks & Spencer only sell free-range eggs in their 285 UK stores (and the 20 stores in France), due to customer demand and the company's sustainability aims in general.

LIGHT GREEN Only buy free-range woodland eggs.

DEEP GREEN Only buy organic milk or yoghurt.

7

EATING OUT

When you eat out, how do you know whether the restaurant, café or pub is serving organic or free-range food? Unless you see very clear signs that the place is trying its best to be sustainable, it probably isn't. Signs saying 'all our meat is organic' or 'all our eggs are free-range' or 'all our cheese is local' mean the company is probably serious about promoting sustainable food and drink.

When you're out with friends and don't want to be a killjoy, it's probably better to go with the flow and not worry if they drag you off to less salubrious places to eat. You can reduce your environmental impact by choosing vegetarian dishes instead of meat or fish dishes (which are unlikely to be sustainably sourced). If you know of a lovely sustainable food restaurant or café, invite your friends along one day – they might like it.

Tap or bottled water?

Do you drink mineral water or tap water when you're out and about? Tap water costs about 0.1p a litre; bottled water about £1 a litre. The UK population spends £2bn a year on bottled water; six million bottles a day. In the UK, bottled water produces around 33,200 tonnes of CO_2 emissions each year, as well as using water, energy and natural resources for its bottling and transportation around the world.

Many people are starting to wake up to the fact that by buying water at 1,000 times the price of tap water, they're contributing huge amounts to the profits of corporations who earn billions each year from bottled water sales. Some bottled water isn't even mineral water – it's from a tap!

The good news is that UK sales of mineral water dropped by 9% in 2007, perhaps a sign that people are starting to see bottled water as the next plastic bag, to be phased out and replaced with a long-life product, like a metal, refillable, bottle for life, available in most camping and outdoor wear shops.

Although plastic bottles can be recycled, most go to landfill, where they take up to 450 years to decompose. The bottle lids are a source of litter and many end up in the sea, where birds and mammals eat them, thinking they're food and slowly die of choking or starvation. Plastic bottles are made from polyethylene terephthalate (PET) plastic.

Recent studies suggest toxins, such as the heavy metal anti-mony, can leach into the water the longer the water stays in the bottle. The detected amounts are small and below current UK safety standards, but with all the other toxic over-loads we encounter in our day-to-day lives, do you want to add another to the cocktail?

LIGHT GREEN If you want to drink filtered water, buy a water filter jug to use at home instead of buying bottled mineral water – you'll save money, too. Make sure you change the filter according to the instructions.

DEEP GREEN Buy a half-litre metal bottle (camping shops, outdoor wear shops and eco-lifestyle shops sell them) that you can keep in your bag and use instead of a plastic bottle.

CALL TO ACTION Start a campaign in your university to stop selling water in plastic bottles and look for other ways of providing students with water:

In the USA, students have joined the Think Outside the Bottle Campaign (www.thinkoutsidethebottle.org) to encourage people to break the plastic bottle habit.

Many institutions already use EcoPure Waters (www.ecopurewaters.com); a water purification system that offers the finest-quality drinking water and reduces bottled water costs by up to 80%.

Beer and wine

Lots of pubs sell local beer on tap, so if you like it, choose it over bubbly bottled foreign beers. Local beer isn't transported very far and is served from the barrel into a glass, so you don't produce glass bottle waste. If wine is your preferred tipple, choose UK or French organic wine, as it's travelled less far than New World wines (reducing CO_2 emissions) and contains fewer chemicals.

As the night wears on and you end up trawling the pubs and clubs, you're probably not in a fit state to think about eco-credentials, but if you're up to it, tell the bartender you don't need straws or cocktail umbrellas. From the bin, straws can find their way into the marine environment and damage marine life. They also use oil in their manufacture.

If you're planning a party or just a relaxing evening at home and you want to get some wine in, spare a thought as to where it's from and how it's made. The best environmental option when buying wine is to buy organic wine produced as near as possible to the point of purchase. Increasing numbers of English and Welsh farmers are growing vines (mainly for white wine). Have a look at the English Wine Producers website (www.englishwineproducers.com).

Most good off-licences and supermarkets, such as Oddbins, Tesco, Sainsbury's, the Co-op and Waitrose, sell organic wine from France and the EU. To check a wine's carbon footprint, go to www.ethicalwine.com. Organic vineyards use natural methods of disease control and maximise crop yields without damaging the environment, and don't cause 'soil desertification' (when intensive farming causes soil to lose its natural structure and nutrients, making it infertile and impossible to grow anything).

Another eco-friendly wine is 'biodynamic' wine, grown following a method pioneered by the Austrian philosopher Rudolf Steiner, based on crop rotation, composting and the rhythmic influence of the sun, moon, planets and stars.

LIGHT GREEN Buy French wine or, as a second best, wine from anywhere in the EU.

DEEP GREEN Only buy organic or biodynamic French wine.

CALL TO ACTION If your local off-licence doesn't sell organic wine, write to the company to ask them what they are doing to improve their sustainable purchasing practices (sourcing French organic wine).

When you buy wine, make sure it's got a natural cork stopper instead of a plastic cork or screw top lid. The use of plastic corks and screw tops is increasing, leading to the abandonment, degradation and loss of one of the world's best eco-systems – the cork forests. If this trend continues, the Western Mediterranean cork oak-growing areas will face economic crises, increases in poverty, intensification of forest fires, a loss of irreplaceable biodiversity and accelerated desertification. This means that the forests could be non-existent by 2016. Cork forests provide a valuable habitat for wildlife, covering about 2.7 million hectares in Portugal, Spain, Algeria, Morocco, Tunisia, Italy and France. The forests support endangered animals such as the Iberian lynx (fewer than 100 breeding pairs left in the world), the Iberian Imperial Eagle; Barbary deer, spiders, toads, geckos, vipers, mongoose, wild cats, boars and genets. They also support millions of migrating birds, including cranes, storks, vultures, buzzards and short-toed eagles.

Cork comes from the bark of the cork oak tree, which is harvested when the tree is 25 years old. More than 15 billion natural cork stoppers are produced each year. Cork provides a source of income for over 100,000 people in Europe and accounts for 70% of the total value of the cork market. The wine industry plays a vital part in maintaining the economic value of cork and the cork oak forests. Fifty per cent of the harvest is used for making wine bottle stoppers; cork is also used for hockey, cricket and golf balls, floor tiles, noticeboards, insulation and boat decking. In addition, acorns from cork trees are used for propagation, animal fodder and cooking oils, the leaves are used for animal fodder and fertiliser, tree cuttings are used for charcoal and firewood and chemicals are made from the natural tannins and acids in the wood.

The good news is that the WWF (www.wwf.org.uk) is campaigning for natural cork – check out their 2006 report online: *Cork Screwed? Environmental and Economic Impacts of the Cork Stoppers Market*. The Co-op supermarket states on its wine bottles whether the stoppers are made from natural cork or not. Cork recycling is established in Portugal and Australia (about 30 tonnes a year) but is rare in the UK.

LIGHT GREEN Buy wine with a real cork stopper instead of a plastic cork or a screw top.

DEEP GREEN Ask your friends to only buy wine with real corks if they're coming to your house for drinks and explain to them why. This will spread the word and hopefully increase the demand for real corks.

CALL TO ACTION Write to the company who owns your off-licence saying you want packaging information on wine bottles saying what type of cork is used.

TOP TIP If you or your friends have barbecues in the summer, corks make great firelighters. You can also compost corks if you have a compost bin.

ECO-MENUS

Eating in is the new eating out! Save money, energy and time by inviting your friends round for a meal. Get them to walk or cycle and reduce CO_2 emissions as well! Here are some suggestions for meals you can make easily and the ingredients are widely available in organic versions in most shops.

Meal 1: The morning after

You are feeling a bit worse for wear but you had a great night out! Now you need a quick no-fuss tasty organic breakfast:

- 1 tin organic baked beans
- 2 slices of wholemeal organic bread (toasted)
- 1 woodland or free range egg (fried or scrambled)
- Fairtrade tea or coffee
- Organic milk
- Organic orange juice.

Meal 2: Broke 'til next week

When you're skint, these cheap, healthy, organic meals will fuel you and keep your brain powered:

- Organic baked beans on organic wholemeal toast
- Woodland or free range scrambled or boiled eggs on organic wholemeal toast
- A bowl of organic cereal with organic milk or yogurt.

Hot date?

Been invited to dinner by the object of your desire? Impress them with ethical chocolate, flowers and wine …

- Make a bouquet of eco-friendly, cheap (but don't mention that part) flowers: buy a small bunch of

UK-grown flowers (look for the Union Jack logo) from the supermarket. Unravel the bunch. Add something green and leafy from the garden (if you have a garden). Arrange the flowers nicely, incorporating the greenery and tie it up with a nice piece of raffia (available from most flower shops).

- Present your beloved (or the one you hope will be) with some Fairtrade chocolates (preferably organic) and support the Fairtrade movement. Fairtrade chocolate is widely available in supermarkets and smaller shops.

- Take along a bottle of organic wine. Most supermarkets sell a decent French organic wine at around £5.

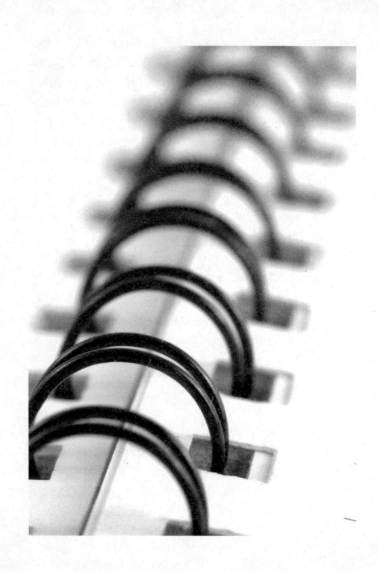

8

STUDYING

STUDY MATERIALS

The main bulk of your study materials will be paper, pens, notepads, books, files and folders. At university you'll be given handouts, lecture notes, workbooks and more. Before long, you'll be staggering under the sheer weight of it all. The natural resources used to make this stuff include trees, water, oil and chemicals, so to reduce your impact on the environment, try to cut down your use of new stationery and buy stationery from sustainable sources.

Notepads

Instead of buying brand-new notepads (lovely, pristine and prettily-coloured though they are), resist: make your own. They don't look as glam but they are cutting-edge. Use unwanted paper that has only been printed on one side and cut it in half, so it's A5-sized. Staple about six sheets together and hey presto – you have a new notepad! If you don't have access to unwanted printer paper, buy notepads made from recycled or FSC paper.

Handouts

If your tutor produces handouts printed only on one side of the paper, ask nicely whether it's possible for them to be printed double-sided. If the answer is 'no' because the printer isn't designed to print double-sided, ask your SU to take up the issue of double-sided printing with the university on your behalf. Some universities make lecture notes and handouts available on the university website (so you can read them online and print them yourself only if necessary).

Pens and pencils

Buy refillable pens and pencils. Buying refills costs less than buying new pens or pencils each time and reduces the amount of plastic waste sent to landfill.

Highlighters, Tipp-ex® and other whiffy things

The aroma of highlighter pens, Tipp-ex® and markers comes from the toxic chemicals in them. Try to buy the non-toxic versions, widely available in stationery shops. Check the labels or ask the shop assistant. If your university sells pens and Tipp-ex® made with toxic substances, contact the Environment Officer or Purchasing Department to ask whether procurement of non-toxic products are included in the tender documentation for stationery contracts. Alternatively, ask your SU to take up the cause on your behalf.

Books

Instead of buying new books, check the library to see if they have what you need on the shelves. The library can order books from other libraries if they don't have them. For novels and non-academic books, check out charity shops or second-hand bookshops. Oxfam's specialist bookshops are full of high-quality second-hand books and Amazon resellers offer a wide range.

You could set up a book swap for expensive academic books, swapping with students on similar courses to yours. It could be virtual; a list of books you want to swap set up on a noticeboard or website where all students will see it.

9

SHOPPING FOR ESSENTIALS

I WANT IT AND I WANT IT NOW

We all know that feeling of wanting something new, whether it's a new pair of jeans, the latest trainers or a CD. In our society, fashion and consumption rules, although more and more people are starting to rethink their values and consider whether material goods make them truly happy. It's amazing how much money you can save by reducing what you buy and reviewing what you already have.

Reducing consumption is a good way to be more eco-friendly but we do have to buy stuff from time to time, even if we're being really frugal. It's good to buy from companies that are doing their bit to help the environment. Some eco-friendly companies and products are mentioned in this book, which may seem like brazen advertising but I've put them in to save you spending hours browsing the Internet.

If you shop on the high street, it can be hard to find eco-friendly products, although some shops are starting to stock them. Unless you live near an 'eco lifestyle' or health-food shop, the only thing you can do is consider alternatives, such as online shopping.

Slim your wardrobe

To work out what clothes you really need to buy, do the 'Slim Your Wardrobe' challenge:

- Gather all your clothes together and separate them into piles of similar clothing, for example T-shirts, trousers, shirts, skirts, tops, socks, underwear.
- Look at the piles. How many pairs of jeans do you own? Do you own three black T-shirts and six white ones? Then you probably don't need any more. Make a note of what you already have so that when you're out shopping you don't spend money needlessly on yet another T-shirt/pair of jeans. If you think you might weaken, make a list to keep with you.
- Give any stuff you no longer want to a friend or charity shop, hold a Swap Shop or sell it on eBay.

Buy Nothing Day

Before you go for your next retail fix, you could take part in 'Buy Nothing Day', an international movement to celebrate one day in the year when we don't buy anything. For 24 hours you can leave consumerism behind and think about the higher things in life. The Buy Nothing Day website (www.buynothingday.co.uk) tells you which date it falls on each year and provides e-cards you can send to friends to advertise the day. Join the Buy Nothing Day Facebook Group (instructions are on the website) and promote the event to your friends and family.

Shopping bags

Take a cloth bag for life (or two or three) with you when you go shopping. At the very minimum, reuse plastic carrier bags; carry a couple with you in your bag or pocket. Some shops put your goods in tissue paper, then into a beautiful bag with ribbon handles and the receipt in a cardboard envelope. It looks lovely but what a waste of natural resources! Just say no to the bag, the tissue paper and the envelope (explain you're trying to reduce waste).

> **TOP TIP** If you're tired out from shopping and fancy a skinny latte and a sandwich, try to find a café that sells Fairtrade tea and coffee (there is a growing number). Some even offer organic milk. By asking 'do you sell Fairtrade tea or coffee?' or 'do you have organic milk?' you are raising the company's awareness that customers are demanding eco-friendly, ethical products.

121

Bedding

If you live in university accommodation or a shared house, you've probably got all the furniture you need but you might want to buy some soft furnishings to make your room more cosy.

People Tree (www.peopletree.co.uk) sells organic duvet covers, sheets and pillow cases made by small communities with a tiny carbon footprint. Organic sheets are not bleached or treated with formaldehyde or other chemicals, which are bad for the environment and human health. It can be difficult to find organic bedding in the High Street, so it's probably better to order online unless there's an eco-home furnishings shop near you.

Paint

If you decide to paint your room (check with your university or landlord first), use eco-friendly paint (available from eco-lifestyle shops or online). If you can't get hold of eco-paint, buy paint with a minimal VOC (volatile organic compounds) content (0–0.29% per gram per litre). These are available in most DIY shops. Avoid paint with VOC levels over 0.29%. VOCs are bad for the environment, because they rise into the atmosphere and destroy the ozone layer, which contributes to global warming. The smell of new paint comes from the VOCs, released as the paint dries. The vapour continues to be released for months or sometimes years after paint is applied. The chemicals evaporate into the air as the paint dries and can cause breathing difficulties, headaches and more serious symptoms, especially when breathed in over long periods, as they contain carcinogens and neurotoxins.

Eco-paint is not only VOC-free but, depending on the brand, may contain natural pigments and sustainable, naturally-derived solvents (such as alcohol and orange oil), be vegetarian-friendly (no animal ingredients), completely free of petrochemicals and titanium dioxide and not tested on animals. The good news is that from 2010, new government regulations will require paint and varnishes to have even lower VOC levels.

Toxins found in non eco-friendly paint can include:

- VOCs
- solvents – white spirit, turpentine, terpenes, ethereal oils, glycols, coalescents
- animal products
- heavy metals, lead, cadmium, mercury
- formaldehyde, acrolein
- vinyl chloride
- phthalates
- APEO (alkylphenol ethoxylates)
- acrylic softeners.

If you have some good-quality paint left over (more than a third of the tin), it could be re-used. Offer it to friends or family or donate it to a local Community RePaint scheme. Community RePaint accepts unwanted, good-quality paint and distributes it to people on low incomes or to community arts projects. Their website (www.communityrepaint.org.uk) will tell you if there's a scheme near you.

If you have to put paint in the dustbin, you must leave it to dry out first, as liquid paint can leach into water-courses. To dry out paint, put the tin in a very safe place, where it won't get kicked over or rained on (outside, in a garden shed or under a lean-to). Leave the lid off and allow the paint to dry out completely, which can take a while. Check by piercing the paint skin. If you need to dispose of paint in your university, contact the Health & Safety Department or Environment Officer, who should be able to give you guidance.

You can buy eco-furnishings and paint online from:

- Ethical Superstore: www.ethicalsuperstore.com
- One Village: www.onevillage.com
- Ecos Organic Paints: www.ecosorganicpaints.com
- Green Paints: www.greenshop.co.uk

PLANTS FOR CLEAN AIR

If you have been painting, or even if you haven't, house-plants can help purify your indoor air. They can absorb up to 60% of formaldehyde and other toxins in the indoor environment. You can get cheap, low-maintenance plants, such as rubber plants, English ivy, spider plants and *Ficus* species (weeping figs) from garden centres.

LIGHT GREEN If you're going to paint your room, use minimal VOC content paint (under 0.29%).

DEEP GREEN Buy your home furnishings from an ethical shop or online supplier.

CALL TO ACTION Your university is likely to use substantial amounts of paint in building refurbishment, repairs and maintenance. Contact the Estates Department (or ask your SU to contact them on your behalf), to ask what the university strategy for reducing the use of toxic paint substances and whether eco-paint (or minimal VOC content) is specified in the tender documents for building contractors and sub-contractors.

ETHICAL BANKING

Before you go shopping, give a thought to your bank account. Ethical banking is important; while you are doing your bit to save the environment, your bank may be working against you by investing in the arms trade or other unethical practices. Major banks that have good ethical investment policies are:

- Triodos Bank (www.triodos.co.uk): Triodos has an online savings account which you can open with as little as £1. Triodos only lends to organisations that really make a difference, from vegetable box companies to organic champions like the Soil Association and green electricity companies like Ecotricity.

- Co-operative Bank (www.co-operativebank.co.uk): the Co-operative Bank doesn't invest in businesses involved in the development of GM crops, the arms trade, the fur trade, businesses whose core activity contributes to climate change through production or extraction of fossil fuels or businesses that fail to uphold human rights.

- Smile (www.smile.co.uk): Smile doesn't invest in businesses that test cosmetics and household products on animals, or lend to manufacturers of harmful chemicals or finance businesses involved in the manufacture or transfer of arms to oppressive regimes.

- Ecology Building Society (www.ecology.co.uk): the Ecology Building Society invests in various ethical and sustainable projects.

If you decide to switch to an ethical bank account, make sure you tell your old bank why you are moving, to raise awareness of the demand for ethical banking.

10

LOOKIN' GOOD

LOTIONS AND POTIONS

Shower gel, shampoo, conditioner, bath oil, make-up, grooming products – the ingredients in our lotions and potions are absorbed into our bodies through our skin. And world-wide, litres of these products are washed down plug-holes and into the sewers every day. Some of the chemicals in these products can't completely be taken out during the sewage filtering process and so eventually get into our drinking water and marine environment. There is some evidence that many of the ingredients found in cosmetics and body cleansers are potentially carcinogenic. Although the levels of toxins are below current safety levels, new evidence suggests that as the chemicals accumulate their impact can be harmful. Perhaps now is a good time to re-think the way we allow toxic chemicals to enter our bodies and opt for non-toxic products.

If you browse the Internet, you'll find information both for and against certain ingredients in cosmetics. Not all the products used in cosmetics today have been widely studied but in the future, if the evidence is there, they may be re-classified as toxic and banned from cosmetics. The question to ask yourself is, do you want to wait to find out? Do you want to wait until conclusive scientific evidence is available or do you want to be a human guinea pig?

Rather than trying to work out exactly what's in your mascara or lipstick, it's easiest to identify which companies produce toxin-free make-up and only buy those. Many companies market their products as 'natural' but under scrutiny, some contain petrol-derived ingredients or other potentially toxic chemicals. If a company's products are certified organic and natural and the list of ingredients are easily available on the company website, they're probably fine.

These brands use certified organic, natural and cruelty-free ingredients. The list is not exhaustive and if you browse the web you'll find lots more:

- Kingfisher (www.kingfishertoothpaste.com) tooth-paste doesn't contain artificial colourings, flavour-ings, preservatives, fluoride, gluten or GM ingredients. It uses natural ingredients like fennel, lemons and peppermint and is cruelty-free. It's available in most supermarkets, health food shops, many chemists and online. British Dental Health Foundation (BDHF) approved.

- Dr Hauschka (www.drhauschka.co.uk) organic make-up and cleansing products are very high quality. All the ingredients for each product are listed on the website, so you can check before you buy them. Products are widely available in health food shops, some chemists and online.

- Neal's Yard (www.nealsyardremedies.com) sells cleansing products, baby products and aromatherapy products. The website lists all ingredients for each product and where they come from. There are 35 stores in the UK or you can order online.

- Aubrey Organics (www.aubreyorganics.co.uk) sells cleansing products, hair dye and household cleansers that are organic and cruelty-free. No petrochemicals. Call 0800 0851 697 to find the nearest stockist or order online.

- Weleda (www.weleda.co.uk) beauty products are organic and cruelty-free. The range includes cleansing products, baby products and toothpaste. Some products are suitable for vegetarians (no lanolin, which is made from sheep's wool). The website provides a full list of ingredients for each product. Available in health food shops, some chemists and online.

- Aveda (www.aveda.co.uk) sells ethically-sourced cosmetics and hair products. There are many stores and outlets in the UK including department stores and hairdressers.

- Borlind, Lavera, Elysambre, Nvey (www.naturisimo. com) sell organic, natural and ethical cosmetics with full lists of ingredients.

- Natural Collection (www.naturalcollection.com) sells cosmetics, household cleansers, clothes and much more.

- Green People (www.greenpeople.co.uk) sells all types of cleansing products.

- Essential Care (www.essential-care.co.uk) sells moisturisers, essential oils, hair and body care.

Top three chemicals to avoid

Paraben: Paraben (or para-hydroxybenzoic acid) is a synthetic petroleum-based chemical added to cosmetics to keep them fresh. Varieties of paraben include methylparaben, propylparaben butylparaben and ethylparaben. Animal tests show that it can cause reproductive and endocrine disruption, kidney failure, brain and nervous system damage and possibly is carcinogenic. It has hormone-disrupting potential and may be responsible for falling sperm counts and rising breast cancer rates in humans. Paraben is found in shampoo, styling gel and mousse, conditioner, tooth-whitening toothpaste, body wash, moisturiser, bath oil and salts, body scrubs and deodorants.

Triclosan: Triclosan is found in deodorants, liquid hand soap, facial cleanser, acne treatment, body wash, moisturiser, toothpaste, lipstick, body spray, antibacterial sponges and cloths. It has restricted use in Canada and Japan. Scientific tests have shown it is accumulating in the environment and it is commonly detected in human and animal tissue. Swedish research published in 2002 found high levels of triclosan in 60% of human breast milk samples. In animal tests, it has been shown to be a hormone and endocrine system disrupter and causes damage to the reproductive system. There is evidence of cancer and thyroid damage in mammals and amphibians in the wild. Companies are not obliged by law to state whether triclosan is in their products, so you won't necessarily know whether it's in a product by looking at the label.

Phthalates: Phthalates are used in many products, including cosmetics and perfumes. On the Internet, you can find lots of information supporting the use of phthalates and statements to say they're not dangerous to humans. But phthalates are the most abundant industrial pollutants in the environment, found in water, soils and sediments. That can't be good, can it? They've even been detected in deep-sea jellyfish and the Antarctic. Tests in animals show evidence of decreased fertility rates, foetal and birth defects, altered hormone levels and uterine damage, and that phthalates cause reproductive and developmental harm. Most products don't have to state whether or not they contain phthalates, so the only way to be sure you're avoiding them is to buy certified natural cosmetic products.

LIGHT GREEN Buy an eco-friendly product when you buy body cleansing products or make-up and gradually add more.

DEEP GREEN Each time you run out of shampoo, conditioner, soap or body scrub, buy an eco-friendly product to replace it.

TOP TIP Did you know you can get eco-friendly accessories? Check out Neal's Yard for organic cotton face flannels; the Body Shop for body brushes made from FSC wood and non-animal-based make-up brushes and bath brushes.

MAKE-UP

This section is for the majority of make-up wearers – women – but if you're a bloke with a penchant for guyliner and manscara, it applies to you, too.

Skin is the body's largest organ, with 60 cm of blood vessels lying beneath every square centimetre; it absorbs up to 60% of the products that are slathered on to it directly into the bloodstream. Even lipstick can find its way in – typically, lipstick or lip balm wearers ingest between 1½ and 4 tubes in their life.

Slim your make-up bag

It's hard to resist the allure of sparkly new make-up. Most people have much more make-up than they actually use. It's better for the environment – and your pocket – to buy less make-up, so do the 'Slim Your Make-up Bag' challenge:

- Collect all your make-up together, including stashes around the house, in drawers, bags or the bathroom.

- Divide it into three piles: make-up you never use or is very old; make-up you have more than one of (for example, three black eyeliners); make-up you use most of the time.

- Throw away all the make-up you never use or is very old (old make-up is an ideal breeding-ground for bacteria, so it's not a good idea to give used unwanted make-up to friends). Some empty make-up containers are recyclable but if not, you'll have to put them in the waste bin.

- Clean up the make-up you have more than one of (sharpen eyeliners and clean pots and brushes). Put in a bag and store for when your current make-up runs out.

- Put the stuff you do use back in your make-up bag.

When your make-up (and reserves) runs out, replace it with eco-friendly make-up. Over time the contents of your make-up bag will become 100% eco-friendly.

LIGHT GREEN Buy at least one item of eco-friendly make-up next time you buy make-up.

DEEP GREEN Replace all your make-up gradually with eco-friendly products.

TOP TIP You can buy eco-friendly make-up brushes that are not made from animal hair, fur or bristle from most companies that sell eco-friendly make-up.

VITAMIN SUPPLEMENTS

You may need vitamin supplements from time to time, especially if you've had too many late nights or are under stress because exams are looming. If you prefer vitamins that are free of animal-derived ingredients, such as gelatine, you can buy Viridian vitamin capsules (various types) from Neal's Yard, which are suitable for vegans and vegetarians. The capsules are free from gluten, wheat, lactose, added sugar, salt, yeast, preservatives or artificial flavouring.

11

CLOTHES

Ethical clothes are clothes that have been made, worn and passed on in a way that looks after people, animals and the environment. Ethical fashion is becoming cool in its own right, slowly making the move from catwalk to high street, with a list of celebrity fans such as Scarlett Johansson, Natalie Portman, Brad Pitt, Leona Lewis and Leonardo di Caprio. Fashion designers and clothing companies are starting to incorporate ethical clothing into their ranges (for example, Gap, New Look and Top Shop).

Although top fashion designers are embracing ethical ideas, it can be hard to find a wide choice of ethical clothes on the average high street, except in shops such as American Apparel. Buying clothes from charity or vintage shops also counts as ethical shopping, because you're reducing the amount of waste sent to landfill. There's a growing demand for ethical clothing, so more shops might sell them in future. If you can't find ethical clothes locally, you can buy them from online companies, such as People Tree, Cotton Roots or The Natural Store. Howies (www.howies.co.uk) is great for tops, hoodies, bags, jackets and much more. For jeans, have a look at the Ethical Consumer website (www.ethicalconsumer.org) and select 'jeans' in the left-hand margin.

Ethical clothing can be a bit more expensive than standard clothes, for good reason – the money goes directly to the workers, so they get a decent wage. They are often high-quality and last well, which is more cost-effective in the long run. Maybe the best option is to buy fewer new clothes and when you do buy, spend a bit more and buy ethical clothes.

The concept of ethical clothes includes at least one of these principles:

- Made and traded sustainably: clothes and accessories made by workers who get a fair wage, guaranteed labour rights and good working conditions and which bring new benefits to communities.

- Sustainable materials: the raw materials needed for the garment are extracted or grown with minimal impact on the environment. Examples include clothes made from organic cotton, which is safer for farmers, garment workers and the environment, because it's free from chemical pesticides and fertilisers; also clothes made from natural materials such as hemp and bamboo (amazingly, bamboo can be made into very soft fabric!).

- Recycled or vintage: keeps clothes out of landfill and reduces fabric waste from factories. Some fashion designers are making clothes from classic vintage items and stylish one-off pieces from recycled garments, factory off-cuts and remnants.

For the latest on eco-fashion and campaigns, sign up to Thread (www.bbc.co.uk/thread), the online ethical fashion magazine.

Campaigning for ethical fashion

Labour Behind the Label (www.labourbehindthelabel.org) runs campaigns for ethical clothing in which you can get involved. Or you can campaign for ethical clothes by signing up to People & Planet's (www.peopleandplanet.org) *Redress Fashion* campaign, which includes making sure university shop merchandise is ethically traded and not from sweatshops.

If you're an outdoors person, you might like Icebreaker (www.icebreaker.com); outdoor clothing made from pure merino wool rather than petroleum-derived materials such as polypropylene or polyester. Icebreaker products are ethically and environmentally sustainable. Through its supply-chain management, it ensures socially and environmentally ethical conditions for all manufacturing and purchases its wool in contracts with the best growers at a premium price.

Icebreaker buys about 20% of New Zealand's merino wool, which has re-ignited its once-flagging merino wool industry. Icebreaker is committed to animal welfare and its suppliers have to operate under strict environmental guidelines and demonstrate they are consciously trying to minimise their environmental impacts, such as reducing their energy consumption and chemical use. The merino sheep used for Icebreaker garments are shorn at the correct time of year, so they don't suffer in New Zealand's extreme temperatures. You can track the origin of your Icebreaker clothes through the 'Baarcode' system (www.icebreaker. com/site/baacode). Just enter your garment code on the website to see photos of the sheep whose wool went into your garment and a description of how they are reared on the farm. UK online suppliers of Icebreaker clothing include Taunton Leisure (www.tauntonleisure.com) and The Mountain Factor (www.themountainfactor.com).

For non-sweatshop-made clothes check out American Apparel (www.americanapparel.co.uk), a company committed to giving its workers a fair wage. The average American Apparel worker makes about $12 or more an hour, which is well over the US federal minimum. Workers have access to subsidised public transport, lunches, free massages, a bike-lending programme, paid days off, study classes, health insurance and much more. Workers have job security, which is typically hard to find in the garment industry, dominated as it is by seasonal work.

People Tree (www.peopletree.co.uk) is a member of IFAT (International Fair Trade Association). Its suppliers have minimal environmental footprints – most of the workers live and work in communities without most 'essentials' of modern life, like electricity, using hand production methods to earn their living. People Tree's policy is to promote natural and organic cotton farming, without using damaging chemicals in the production process and to use recycled and biodegradable substances where possible. The production process also protects water supplies and forests in the environment where workers work.

Cotton Roots (www.cottonroots.co.uk) sells fabulous organic and Fairtrade clothes, especially bright coloured T-shirts and hoodies and often has good discounts on end-of-line clothing. The Natural Store's (www.naturalcollection.com) products include 'EcoSneaks' which are trainers made from recycled materials such as leather from car seats, seatbelts, bicycle tyres and recycled rubber (although you'd never know by looking at them). They cost about £60.

DO A CLOTHES SWAP!

As well as buying ethical clothes, reducing the amount we send to landfill is important. It's estimated that over 7.5 billion items of clothing (about one million tonnes) are thrown away in the UK each year. Swapping, borrowing and buying vintage clothes are all great ways to reduce clothing waste, save money and reduce the pollution caused by the clothing manufacturing industry. Pollution from clothing waste is a serious issue: dyes, chemicals and bleaches from discarded clothes leach into the ground when it rains and can contaminate water supplies. Once groundwater is contaminated, it's almost impossible to decontaminate. Also, when biodegradable clothes (those made from wool and cotton) decompose in landfill, they produce methane, which contributes to global warming.

So, stop buying and start swapping. Save the environment and re-invent your wardrobe for free – organise a clothes swap. Tell your friends (at least the ones with good taste) that you are holding a clothes swap party. Ask everyone to bring at least one item of clothing, pair of shoes or accessory. Lay out all the items on the floor, beds or sofas so everyone can see what's up for grabs. Each person can take whatever they want and any remaining clothes can be taken to the local charity shop. To find a charity shop near you, go to www.charityshops.org.uk.

University swap shop

Imagine a university where stuff was free – clothes, DVDs, CDs, books, bags and furnishings for your room. It's true you can sell unwanted stuff on eBay or give it away on Freecycle but wouldn't it be great if you had a way to circulate good-quality, unwanted items within your university? Set up regular swap shops – it's easy to do. You need a big room, a few tables to display items and about six volunteers to run the event. Offer (Fairtrade) tea, coffee and biscuits and put on some music to add to the celebratory feeling.

Make sure you get permission from staff – and involve them for help with the logistics. You'll be amazed at the good-quality items people bring to swap shops – and think of the money you'll save on not having to buy new.

For ideas on how to run a Swap Shop in your university, have a look at the University of Oxford Swap Shop Guide (www.admin.ox.ac.uk/estates/environment/waste/swap-shop.pdf).

You could consider persuading your university to set up a 'virtual' swap shop on a noticeboard or website, where students can advertise clothes they want to swap (or simply give away). A brilliant example of a swap shop website is 'Swap It Surrey', developed by Surrey County Council (www.surreywaste.info/swapitsurrey).

Beg, borrow or steal

Well, perhaps not steal – and begging might be beneath you – but you could borrow clothes from your friends if they trust you to take care of them. Promise to return them promptly soon after you've worn them. And do it!

Stitch 'n' Bitch

Probably more people in universities can programme a computer than can create their own clothes. The skill of mending clothes has largely been lost and we often buy new when our clothes get damaged. Although making clothes from scratch might be a bit extreme, some things can be mended with the right tools: needle and cotton or sewing machine. Share your mending skills and tools with fellow students and set up a *Stitch 'n' Bitch* club. Sewing machines are expensive but club members could chip in or you could buy a second-hand machine or ask relatives to donate one.

PROLONG THE LIFE OF YOUR CLOTHES

The long-term maintenance of your clothes has an impact on the environment: dry cleaning, washing and ironing all use energy, water and chemicals.

To make the whole process of looking after clothes more eco-friendly, try to buy clothes that don't need ironing or cut down on ironing things like underwear, jeans and duvet covers (you'll also save energy and have more time to study and play!). When washing clothes, remember a 60°C wash uses at least 30% more energy than a 30°C wash. Most clothes, unless they're very dirty, can be washed at 30°C.

Non eco-friendly detergents and fabric conditioners contain chemicals such as surfactants that are toxic to the marine environment, so use eco-friendly brands, such as Ecover. Eco-friendly detergents don't have bactericides, so after a few months of using them, bacteria can build up in the washing machine, causing it to smell. This is easy to remedy – use a standard detergent once a month at 90°C in an empty wash cycle (if you live in shared accommodation pin a calendar on the wall to remind you). This prevents bacterial build-up in the machine and means you can use eco-friendly detergent for the rest of the month.

Stains

Rub stained garments with hand soap or soak for a couple of hours in soapy water before washing them. If you do need to use a stain remover, use an eco-friendly brand, such as Ecover.

Dry-cleaning

Dry-cleaning uses chemicals derived from petroleum, is very expensive and is best avoided. Perchloroethylene, a common dry-cleaning chemical, is a known animal carcinogen and probable human carcinogen. It's also a neuro-toxin and linked to liver and kidney illness. Obviously some clothes have to be dry-cleaned, for example, tailored suits or coats, but if you don't buy clothes that need to be dry-cleaned, especially everyday ones like shirts, jumpers, trousers and skirts, you'll save the environment, your money and the hassle of having to spend time taking them to the shop.

It's not unusual to see 'dry clean only' on clothing labels made from materials, such as cotton or silk, that traditionally are very durable and really don't need to be dry-cleaned. Some retailers say that because the clothing industry is global and consequently it's harder to track clothing quality assurance, manufacturers are increasingly putting 'dry clean only' labels on their clothes, because they can't guarantee the effect of washing clothes in water. You can try washing 'dry clean only' everyday clothes (shirts and skirts, for example) by hand in cold water: it's eco-friendly, but if the garment shrinks you can't return it to the shop, so it can be risky.

Some dry-cleaners are looking into alternative cleaning fluids: for example, computerised 'wet cleaning' using water and biodegradable soap. This is a non-toxic dry-cleaning method that controls agitation and humidity levels to prevent shrinking. Until all dry-cleaners switch to this method, it's better to avoid 'dry clean only' clothes.

TOP TIP If you do take clothes to the dry-cleaners, return the hangers and plastic covering on your next visit, for re-use or recycling. If the shop doesn't recycle, return them anyway, in the hope that you'll encourage them to start. While you're there, ask them if they are considering switching to more eco-friendly dry-cleaning methods.

CALL TO ACTION If your favourite shop sells lots of clothes that say 'dry clean only' on the label, write to the company and ask them what it is doing to phase out 'dry clean only' clothes and become more eco-friendly.

12

HOW CLEAN IS YOUR HOUSE?

You've probably got better things to do than clean your house, but as cleaning products can be both toxic and a source of environmental pollution, you need to know how to reduce your reliance on them when you do get round to it. Most seemingly-harmless cleaning products contain chemicals that are gradually building up in the environment, polluting our drinking water and affecting our health and the marine environment.

The alternative is eco-friendly products, made from renewable plant and mineral ingredients, rather than petrochemicals. They biodegrade completely, so they don't persist in the environment. Genuine eco-friendly detergents don't contain foam boosters, which are damaging to the environment; phosphates, which starve rivers of oxygen and suffocate wildlife; or artificial scents made from petrochemicals, which are increasingly found in the body tissue of many species of fish – including fish we eat – due to chemical build-up in our water systems and seas.

So ditch the toxins. All the products you'll ever need to keep your house clean and toxin-free are:

- Bucket for water to clean the floor/toilet (keep separate from washing-up bowl!)
- Two cloths – one for floor, one for surfaces
- Two scouring cloths – one for floor, one for surfaces
- Dustpan and brush
- Vacuum cleaner
- Multi-purpose cleaner (Ecover or Bio-D are good products)
- White vinegar (dilute 50/50 with water) & newspaper for cleaning windows
- Toilet cleaner (Ecover toilet cleaner or similar eco-brand).

Ecover eco-friendly detergents are widely sold in supermarkets and shops. The range covers shower gel, hand soap, washing-up liquid, washing liquid, toilet cleaner, surface cleaner and more. Online suppliers of Ecover have a larger range, including car-washing detergents, limescale remover and air fresheners. Suppliers of Ecover include Ecotopia and Ecoretail Online (www.ecotopia.co.uk or www.ecoretail-online.com). Other brands of eco-detergent to look out for include the Bio-D range and Earth Friendly products. You can buy them online at www.ethicalsuperstore.com and from some Oxfam shops and health food shops.

The e-cloth (www.e-cloth.com) is a cloth that doesn't need detergent to clean. The e-cloth is made of microfibre and cleans surfaces without scratching. To get surfaces sparkly clean, you need only use water.

If you have bottles of old cleaning products in the cupboard that you no longer use, don't pour them down the sink or toilet, as that defeats the object of trying to save the environment by using eco-friendly products. Bleach is particularly nasty and you should avoid using it at all. Screw the lids on tightly, put the containers in a plastic bag and ask your council or university if they can dispose of them responsibly. Your university's Safety Office may be able to give you advice on chemical disposal.

TOP TIP It's easy to buy too many cleaning products when you share a house; everyone does their own shopping and no one really checks what's under the sink. To save money and time, write a list of the cleaning products you already have and pin it on the wall. When a product runs out make sure whoever buys the replacement buys Ecover or a similar eco-friendly brand.

13

NATURE

Nature is so much more than trees and green spaces; it provides natural resources crucial for our survival. It's a wonder that the leaders of the world have allowed finite materials to deplete to the extent they have. Nature provides us with oil, gas, trees for timber and CO_2 absorption, animals and plants for pharmaceuticals and food, natural filtering systems for clean water, pollinating insects, building materials, pest control … the list is endless.

Governments' constant desire for growth in the name of the economy is pushing nature to its limits. It's physically impossible for an economy to keep growing if it surpasses the Earth's biophysical limits. The trouble with unchecked consumerism and development is that we're using up our natural resources and damaging nature in the process.

Another way of describing the destruction of wildlife and wildlife habitats is 'biodiversity decline'. It's crucial that we halt biodiversity decline, both in the UK and globally. Some

universities are trying to prevent further decline by improving wildlife habitats in their own grounds, for example by using 'green' roofs on new buildings, planting trees that produce flowers and berries for wildlife and buying timber from certifiably sustainably-managed forests.

According to the International Union for the Conservation of Nature, one in four mammal species is at risk of becoming extinct in the near future: 1,141 of the 5,487 mammal species on Earth. At least 76 mammal species have become extinct since 1500. However, thanks to world-wide wildlife conservation work, 5% of currently-threatened mammals are showing signs of coming back from the brink of extinction.

Bees

Animals are part of the human food chain. We don't know what will happen if a vast number of species become extinct but let's take just one – the bumblebee – which pollinates food crops world-wide. Einstein said: 'If the bee disappeared off the surface of the globe then man would only have four years of life left'.

Einstein understood that we need bees to produce food. In the UK, bees pollinate £200 million worth of food crops a year. Apart from their economic benefits, bees are a 'keystone' species; if they disappear, many other species will disappear with them. About a third of plants in the UK are pollinated mainly by bees (but also other insects). Bees don't like chemicals and they love wild flowers, so the best way to support them is to buy organic food. Organic food production emphasises growing wild flowers, using natural pest control, creating wildlife habitats and avoiding the use of harmful chemicals, all of which is good news for bees and other pollinating insects. Another problem for bees is Colony Collapse Disorder (CCD), which is wiping out bee colonies all over the world. No one knows for sure what causes CCD or how to cure it, but agricultural chemicals, intensive bee farming and climate change are thought to contribute. Bees used for mass-producing honey or large-scale pollination are often fed with synthetic sugars, which is not as good for them as natural pollen from flowers and may weaken their immune systems. These bees' hives are in huge artificial colonies, stacked high, which encourages the spread of disease.

There are 256 bee species in the UK but 25% of them are on the international endangered species list, due to a decline in wild flowers, intensive farming, the paving-over of gardens and building development. Bees are increasingly dependent on gardens for pollen, so if you have a garden, create a bee-friendly environment: plants such as buddleia, sedum, lavender, rosemary and mint are loved by bees and easy to grow.

Bees are very sensitive creatures. They are intelligent, have memories and use visual orientation to estimate accurately their distance from a nectar source. They are master architects, constructing hives that keep warm in winter and cool in summer. By supporting organic farming and creating bee-friendly habitats, we can help reverse the damage which is taking its toll on these important creatures.

LIGHT GREEN Only buy organic honey from UK or EU producers.

DEEP GREEN Write to the government to ask that more money is allocated to finding out why bee populations are dying out (see template letter at the back of the book to save time).

CALL TO ACTION To help protect biodiversity:

- Buy paper and timber products that are recycled and/or FSC certified (helps to stop rainforest destruction).
- Buy organic food (uses fewer pesticides and herbicides which harm wildlife and the marine environment).
- Buy products made in the UK (reduces CO_2 emissions from transport).
- Use eco-friendly washing detergents and body cleansing products (reduces pollution in the marine environment).

- Grow plants that attract bees and butterflies (buddleia, thyme, rosemary and mint) or if you don't have a garden, encourage your family/friends to plant some.

- Create mini-wildlife habitats – stuff some dry plant stems and stalks into an old flowerpot and put it in a quiet, sheltered place where there's some sun – insects will hibernate there.

- Put water out for the birds (change it every two days). A shallow container is best, large enough for birds to bathe in.

VOLUNTEERING FOR BIODIVERSITY

Volunteering for conservation projects, both in the UK and abroad, is an excellent way to get hands-on experience of protecting wildlife and habitats. BTCV (www.btcv.org. uk) is a nature conservation organisation that runs hundreds of voluntary projects for people who want to take practical action to improve their urban and rural environments. There are currently 140,000 volunteers working on BTCV projects.

BTCV runs Green Gym sessions in which volunteers work on an area to make it more wildlife-friendly. You work at your own pace and can have a rest, a chat or a cuppa whenever you like. Most Green Gyms work with local councils and landowners to manage scrubland and woodland to benefit wildlife and the local community. Some Green Gyms are based in allotments and urban wildlife areas.

BTCV also runs conservation holidays in the UK and the rest of the world. Check out the website (www.btcv.org/conshols/brochure.html) for more information on what kind of holiday you could have.

How can my university protect biodiversity?

Many universities are developing Biodiversity Action Plans (BAPs). A BAP can extend into many different areas in the university, such as Purchasing, Catering and Estates, because nature's resources are used in almost everything, from paper and timber to parks and landscaping. The EAUC website (www.eauc.org.uk) has information on how to improve biodiversity in universities.

As well as conserving wildlife habitat locally (for example, university grounds), a BAP should also consider building and construction materials which should be procured from sustainable sources, for example: timber from sustainably-managed forests, stone and granite from the UK or EU, peat-free compost and wildlife-friendly plants and trees.

Contact your Environment Officer to find out what your university is doing to reduce its impact on the natural environment or ask your SU to make enquiries on your behalf. Campaign, via the SU, for a university BAP with a clearly-defined implementation plan and targets. If you're campaigning for a university BAP, you may want to include a business argument for why your university should protect biodiversity. The Business and Biodiversity website (www.businessandbiodiversity.org) contains lots of useful information on how to present your case.

CALL TO ACTION Campaign for your university to develop a BAP. If it already has one, find out what the targets are and start a student campaign (via the SU) to take action and work towards the BAP goals, which may include issues such as not buying products containing palm oil (palm oil plantations are being developed over rainforest areas, destroying large amounts of forest forever), buying FSC or recycled paper and timber products, buying eco-friendly cleaning products and serving fish from sustainable stocks.

Sustainable purchasing

Sustainable purchasing (sometimes called sustainable procurement) is a powerful way of protecting biodiversity. Universities and individuals can contribute, both locally and globally, by developing a policy on procuring goods and services for the university that have minimal impacts on biodiversity and the environment in general. Examples of sustainable purchasing include:

- Buying recycled/FSC paper, timber and timber products
- Buying fish from sustainably managed stocks

- Buying organic, locally-reared and -slaughtered meat (or buying less meat)
- Buying eco-friendly cleaning detergents
- Buying eco-friendly stationery (for example, high-lighters, correction fluid).

Even from these few examples, you can see that if all the universities in the UK applied these practices, their impact on the environment would be considerably reduced. Other areas where purchasing can reduce environmental impacts include:

- Working with suppliers to persuade them to adopt more eco-friendly production and transportation processes
- Encouraging staff to adopt more eco-friendly purchasing practices
- Including sustainability in all tender documents, including whole life costing, waste minimisation and pollution prevention when evaluating suppliers' bids
- Specifying the use of eco-friendly materials and products in contracts
- Developing measuring and monitoring tools to measure the sustainable purchasing targets
- See the EAUC website for downloadable guidelines on sustainable procurement.

14

TRAVEL

DAY-TO-DAY TRAVEL

Some universities don't allow students to bring cars to university: roads are becoming more crowded, parking is increasingly expensive and air pollution is a growing problem. Talk to your university Travel Officer about sustainable travel options and incentives for students. Many universities have excellent travel plans to help staff and students travel in ways that have the least impact on the environment, such as walking or cycling (which also keep you fit). If you use a car every day, consider switching to a more sustainable form of transport (perhaps once a week to start with if you're not used to cycling or walking). Remember, 'be seen if you cycle'; wear a fluorescent jacket and get some bike lights (it's illegal to cycle without them!).

If it's too far to walk or cycle, you might be able to use public transport or car-share if you have to drive. If you travel by train and want to cycle to the station, check whether the train company will allow bikes on the train; not all do. If you frequently travel by train and bike, the best bike to buy is the *Brompton*, which meets all the train companies' size, weight and folding standards; it folds up so you can take it on as 'luggage'. Bromptons cost around £500 but could be a worthwhile investment if you can afford it.

A to B Magazine (www.atob.org.uk) contains lots of useful information on types of bikes and travelling by train and bike.

Commonwheels

Buckingham New University has teamed up with the not-for-profit charity Commonwheels (www.commonwheels. org.uk) to launch an on-campus green car club as part of the university's travel plan, which is supported by Wycombe District Council. The club aims to cut down on single-person car trips (and the need to own a second car), reduce CO_2 emissions and provide more travel options for staff and students. Each member of the club will save about 0.7 tonnes of CO_2 emissions per year. The green car club has two low emission VW Polos, which do 70 miles to the gallon. The club cars are available for business use by university staff between 8am and 6pm, Monday to Friday. Outside these hours, the cars can be hired by employees and students for personal use.

TRAVELLING ABROAD

Most people know by now that flying is a no-no and produces high levels of CO_2 emissions. Between three and four thousand planes are flying over Europe as you read this. Aircraft are the fastest-growing polluters, and in the UK account for around 6% of greenhouse gas emissions. But sometimes the desire to feel the sun on our bodies after eight months of British winter is overwhelming, so we jet off to the sunny South of France, Spain or further afield. At the moment it's cheaper to fly than to travel by train, although rising oil prices and the need to reduce CO_2 emissions may mean cheap air travel won't be around for much longer. At the moment, air travel is highly subsidised and there's no tax on aviation fuel, which means flights are cheap. This too may change if the UK gets serious about reducing its flight-related CO_2 emissions.

If your budget is restricted and you only have a week's holiday, taking a train, say, to Greece may not be practical, but if you limit your flights to one a year instead of two or three, you'll reduce your CO_2 emissions. You could use any other holidays to explore England, Scotland, Wales and Ireland. As they say, a change is as good as a rest …

Some people 'offset' flights they can't avoid taking, although this is somewhat controversial, as it can be a 'get out of jail free card' – that is, you continue to pollute but feel less guilty about it because you've paid into an offsetting scheme. Ideally, offsetting should only be considered if you have no choice but to fly. Companies that provide offsetting include www.climatecare.org and www.carbonneutral.com.

HOLIDAYS

There are other things than flying to think about when you go on holiday. Sustainable travel means considering our eco-footprint in terms of pollution, the communities we visit, our use of natural resources and our impact on biodiversity. When you're on holiday, where does your litter go? Do water sports, such as diving and boating, harm marine life? What happens when your sun lotion washes into the sea? Are the souvenirs you buy made from endangered species or come from fragile habitats?

The tourism industry has woken up to the fact that eco-conscious people want to reduce their environmental impact while on holiday and give something back to the local community. B&Bs, campsites and hotels all over the world are switching to eco-friendly practices such as washing towels only when needed, using eco-friendly detergents, low-energy light bulbs and providing organic food and local produce.

Five ways to reduce your eco-footprint on holiday

- Take a bag for your litter if you go to the beach or for a country walk. Some people even spend a few minutes picking other people's litter up. This may not sound like an ideal holiday but if you're bored with lying on the beach, take a ten minute stroll and pick up a few discarded plastic bottle lids or some nylon string so they can't harm marine animals. Keep something heavy on top of your bag so it doesn't get blown away. On a beach it's easy to lose track of bits of paper, plastic bags, water bottles, lids and tissues.

- Don't contribute to the increasing amount of harmful plastic that pollutes beaches and harms marine life. There's an area of plastic twice the size of Texas swirling around in the North Pacific Ocean (see the videos on *YouTube*), the result of people and industry chucking plastic waste in the sea. There are six kilos of plastic for every kilo of plankton and it's estimated that over a million seabirds and 100,000 marine mammals and sea turtles are killed each year by it.

- Try to limit your chemical pollution of the environment. Each time you go swimming, any creams on your skin wash off. These chemicals can harm marine life, so use an eco-friendly product such as Green People's *No Scent* sun lotion (SPF22) or Weleda and Dr Hauschka products. Keep mosquitoes away with Neal's Yard Remedies *Organic Lavender Essential Oil* or *Neem Oil.*

- Don't buy souvenirs that contribute to species extinction, animal cruelty or deforestation. It's nice to buy fascinating objects as presents for friends or to adorn our houses; it's good to boost the local economy but not at the expense of the environment. When you're shopping for presents, never buy souvenirs made from shell, fur, teeth, bone, feathers, ivory, coral, wood (unless it's genuinely certified FSC or sustainably-sourced wood), fossils or plant-based products.

- If you have a television or an empty mini-bar in your B&B or hotel room, turn them off at the socket when you're not using them (don't leave them on standby).

TOP TIP Don't succumb to that sinking feeling of wondering whether or not you left the iron on as you're en route to your holiday destination. Make a point of switching off all electrical appliances and anything in standby mode. Unplug your PC, games consoles and mobile phone chargers. If you're going away for more than two weeks, clear out, defrost and turn off the fridge.

The one-day holiday

Register for Beachwatch (www.adoptabeach.org.uk) and work with hundreds of other volunteers for just one day a year to help clear beaches of litter such as cotton buds, cigarette butts, plastic, rope and netting which, if left, can damage or kill marine wildlife. Beachwatch is an environmental coastal initiative organised by the Marine Conservation Society (MCS) and takes place once a year, usually around the third weekend of September.

Eco-holidays

Whether you're planning to stay in a hotel, a B&B or a yurt in a field, ask to see their environmental credentials, such as their environmental policy, before you decide (most sustainable locations have a summary of their credentials on their webpage). Some places are more eco-friendly than others: use your judgement. You can find sustainable holiday destinations on websites that promote sustainable tourism, such as:

- Responsible Travel (www.responsibletravel.com): Hundreds of eco-holidays in the UK and abroad, from hotels to camp sites. You get a free Rough Guide book of your choice when you book a holiday through them.

- Loco2 (www.loco2travel.com): For people who want low-carbon travel options.

- BTCV (www.btcv.org): Visit somewhere you've never been and meet new people who are eco-minded like you. BTCV conservation holidays are for volunteers who want to combine a holiday with doing something useful and physical. Wash the stress of exams away, visit some beautiful scenery and come back with a sense of achievement. On BTCV holidays you spend the day working with your team of volunteers but have free time in the evenings to relax, socialise and explore the local area.

- WWOOF (www.wwoof.org): 'World Wide Opportunities on Organic Farms'. Volunteers who go 'Wwoofing' work on farms that are either organic, converting to organic or use ecologically sound methods on their land. When you're WwooFing you get hands-on experience of organic farming, country living and an ecological lifestyle. You work for free for a number of hours agreed with your host and they provide you with free accommodation and food.

- Couch Surfing (www.couchsurfing.com): Couch Surfing is much more than just a free place to stay when travelling; it's an international network of people who want to travel and make connections worldwide. Friendships made through Couch Surfing help to create a better world by enabling educational exchanges, raising collective consciousness and spreading tolerance and cultural understanding. Sign up for a free couch and amazing adventures with your global family!

- Sunseed (www.sunseed.org.uk): Sunseed Desert Technology in Almeria, South of Spain, is a project investigating zero-carbon-producing farming solutions in very arid conditions. Volunteers are required to work for a certain number of hours a day in return for food and lodging. There are lots of different projects going on at Sunseed at any one time, so you can gain new skills to do with living sustainably. Activities include gardening, building and general running of the house. Sunseed is powered by zero and low carbon energy. Find out about the challenges of desert agriculture. Download a volunteer application pack from the website.

- Wild Camping (www.go4awalk.com): Wild camping is free. It involves camping in open countryside, not in a campsite. Most land in the UK is cultivated in some way or another so not great for wild camping but there are some good places, such as high in the Lake District Hills, North Wales and the Highlands of Scotland (but not near Loch Ossian or Glen Muick). There are no rules for wild camping but it does have its own etiquette (some of these apply to normal camping, too). Lighting fires is not advisable: farmers don't want fires on their land, there's not usually much wood in the mountains anyway and you should not cut or damage trees. Fires can damage wildlife habitats, destroy ground vegetation which can take many years to recover (if ever) and create an eyesore. If you have to cook, use a stove. Be discreet: put your tent up late and leave early. If you're near a house, ask for permission before you camp. Carry a trowel and bury your poo – don't leave an 'interesting' sculpture for the next camper to contemplate. Take all your litter with you (but if it's raw food that degrades very quickly, such as apple cores, you can leave them in a sheltered place for animals to eat). Never pick flowers or disturb wildlife. Don't pretend you're a survivalist hunting for food: take your food and water with you. Smokers should take extra care with ash and cigarette butts when travelling through environmentally-sensitive areas. Butts contain nasty chemicals and can cause forest or bush fires. Carry a *Boodie* eco-ashtray with you (www.buttsandgum. co.uk); it folds away into a neat little box you can keep in your pocket.

LIGHT GREEN Swap one of your holidays abroad for a UK holiday.

DEEP GREEN Use one of your annual holidays to do voluntary work, such as WwooFing or wildlife conservation.

TOP TIP The Ethical Superstore (www.ethicalsuper-store.com) sells lots of eco-equipment for camping, from biodegradable tent pegs made from potato starch to high-tech sleeping bags made from recycled fabric and insulation.

15

GREEN-COLLAR JOBS

The future is bright green for students who want to develop a career in which they can make a real difference to the environment. Green careers are on the rise. Environmental or 'green-collar' jobs cover a huge range of professions, from energy assessors and hybrid car engineers to carbon footprint calculators. The third sector (Non-Governmental Organisations, local authorities, charities and not-for-profit organisations) also features strongly, with jobs ranging from wildlife monitors in Kenya to university Environmental Officers.

The demand for environmental skills is growing. Environmental jobs were quite rare in the 1980s; now they are part of twenty-first-century life. More and more companies are realising that they have to demonstrate environmental responsibility and meet the increasing amount of legislation, which is good news for students. At the time of writing, the UK is a little behind Germany, Denmark and

Spain, who are creating thousands of green-collar jobs and billions of Euros of revenue. Germany's renewable energy sector employs half a million people, with a turnover of 24 billion, while the UK employs only 7,000 in renewable energy, generating 360 million. The good news is that as the UK catches up, lots of new eco-jobs will be created. Typically, environmental jobs cover: building and construction, design, energy, finance, management, materials, NGOs, policy and planning, transport, and waste and water services.

GREEN YOUR CV

As environmental issues enter the mainstream of business, any environmental experience you gain at university will be useful whichever career path you choose. Even if you don't work in a specifically environmental job, you'll still need to know about business-related environmental corporate responsibility; senior executives need to understand the impact of environmental risk on their business, because stakeholders and shareholders demand it, while purchasing directors need to manage their supply chains to ensure the company reduces waste, pollution and energy consumption and costs.

Volunteering and internships are excellent opportunities for gaining experience in environmental matters, meeting like-minded people and earning a glowing reference in return for your hard work. The environmental profession is one of the fastest-changing areas of business; when you start looking for a job, you'll need to demonstrate you can adapt to different working challenges and environments.

To enhance your CV, you could consider becoming a member of the Institute for Environmental Management and Assessment (IEMA, www.iema.net) – a highly-regarded institute for environmental professionals. Most environmental job advertisements ask for evidence of IEMA membership. Your university may already subscribe to the IEMA journal, so you can browse copies in the Library before deciding whether or not to join. The journals are very informative and contain lots of opportunities for continuing professional development.

Volunteering

Even if you have a degree in an area of environmental management, you still need a competitive edge over your peers. Volunteering and internships during holidays or gap year can be a really useful way of getting hands-on work experience. Working for free may not appeal to everyone but voluntary work has its benefits: it'll look good on your CV and your potential employer will be impressed by your aptitude and go-getting nature. If you volunteer for work that is similar to the career you want to follow, you'll pick up valuable skills that will impress employers, who like to see evidence that students have practical experience as well as having studied the theory.

Some volunteering opportunities are listed in the 'Holidays' section of this book. The following websites advertise paid jobs as well as voluntary opportunities:

- Do.it.org (www.do-it.org.uk): Database of voluntary organisations.

- Frontier (www.frontier.ac.uk): Charity dealing with conservation and development volunteering.

- TravelAid (www.travelaid.org.uk): Oxford student-run charity offering students the chance to volunteer abroad.

- The Royal Society for the Protection of Animals (www.rspca.org.uk).

- The Royal Society for the Protection of Birds (www.rspb.org.uk).

- Earthwatch (www.earthwatch.org).

- Business Environment Partnership (www.thebep. org.uk): Actively recruits and matches students to environmental projects with businesses throughout Scotland through its environmental placement programme.

- Waste Aware Scotland (www.wasteawarescotland. org.uk): Information on current vacancies and volunteering opportunities.

- Volunteer Scotland (www.volunteerscotland.org.uk):

Directory of volunteering opportunities including environment projects.

Google 'environmental groups' in your local area to see if they have volunteering opportunities. Your local council might be able to provide you with a list of groups in your area.

Websites featuring environmental jobs available in the engineering, building and construction sectors include:

- ENDS (www.endsjobsearch.co.uk)
- EDIE (www.edie.net).

Websites with a broad range of environmental jobs including local authorities and not-for-profit organisations and some voluntary placements include:

- Environment Jobs (www.environmentjobs.com)
- Environment Job (www.environmentjob.co.uk)
- Guardian Jobs (jobs.guardian.co.uk).

Internships

The Ethical Fashion Forum (www.ethicalfashionforum. com) offers internships to creative types who want to get experience in the ethical fashion business.

The Soil Association Organic Apprenticeship Scheme

(www.soilassociation.org) is for people who choose not to take a formal educational route into food and farming. The apprenticeship aims to provide a broad understanding and practical experience of farming in relation to twenty-first-century farming challenges such as climate change, energy supplies and organic food.

Your university may offer formal or informal internships to students interested in environmental and sustainability issues. Departments that may be interested include the Estates Department or Purchasing Department (there may also be other departments interested). Ask your tutors whether they can help you identify potential internships or email the relevant departments on your behalf. Or you could approach your university's Environment Committee.

16

FUN AND GAMES

There are many ways to have fun that don't involve messing up the planet. By making small changes, you can party from noon to sunrise and reduce your environmental footprint at the same time.

CELEBRATIONS

Parties are, by their nature, over-indulgent affairs. Drink, eat and be merry but try to consume food, drink and goodies that have a low environmental impact. If you have a finger buffet instead of a sit-down meal, you won't have to wash up plates and cutlery, saving energy and time. Eco-food for a party could include organic:

- Bagels, spread with cream cheese and sprinkled with home-grown chives, cut into segments that are bite-sized

- Cake, cut into bite-sized cubes (not a crumbly cake – a moist fruit cake would work best)
- Crisps, such as Jonathan Crisps
- Wine or beer.

And serve tap water, with slices of lemon and ice cubes, rather than bottled mineral water.

Use 'real' crockery and cutlery but if you don't have enough, buy recyclable or compostable paper plates and cups, rather than polystyrene or plastic plates and cups. If you hold regular parties, invest in glasses that you can use again and again, which is cheaper than buying disposable plates and cups each time you party. Your local pub or supermarket might hire out wine glasses: you'll only pay for the ones you break.

The day after (once your hangover has gone), keep the eco theme going:

- Use Ecover washing-up liquid to wash up all the plates and glasses.
- If people bring six-packs of beer, cut up the plastic rings that hold the cans together before you put them in the waste or recycling bin. Plastic rings may get blown away during rubbish collection and can choke or entangle wildlife.
- Recycle everything you can (glass bottles, plastic

bottles, tin cans, paper or plastic cups). Just give them a quick rinse in the used washing-up water.

• If you have a compost bin, compost all the food and the dirty paper plates.

Balloons add festivity to a party but they're party poopers for wildlife. They look lovely for a few hours but if they escape, the effect on wildlife can last for months. About 90% of escapee balloons rise to an altitude of five miles, where they burst into small fragments due to low temperature and pressure but the remaining 10% drift in the air before falling into the sea, semi-inflated. Balloons have been discovered in the stomachs of many marine creatures (including dolphins, turtles and sharks); these animals can mistake balloons for jellyfish or squid. Semi-inflated balloons can block the pyloric valve (between the stomach and intestines) so food cannot pass through, causing slow, painful starvation.

Balloons don't break down in an animal's stomach: in tests, it took four months for balloons to pass through turtles' digestive systems; not only that, the balloons came out *en masse* and not broken down at all. Some balloons are made of latex, which degrades over several months but many are made of mylar foil, which persists much longer in the environment. The attachments on balloons – ribbons and string – are also a problem, as they get entangled in animals' bodies and mouths.

LIGHT GREEN Buy at least two items for your party that have eco-credentials (for example, organic cheese or French organic wine).

DEEP GREEN Minimise waste by using 'real' glasses and crockery or recyclable paper plates instead of plastic substitutes.

CALL TO ACTION If your university uses balloons to promote festivities, contact the Environment Officer or SU to ask whether it's possible to develop a no-balloons policy for the university. Mention the reasons why balloons are dangerous to wildlife and livestock and that the Marine Conservation Society, the RSPCA and the National Farmers Union are all against them.

The MCS (www.mcsuk.org) is very active in this area and may be able to provide your university with advice and facts on balloon pollution.

Christmas (and other festivities)

Christmas (and other festivities) can be pretty hectic but it's nice to have a break, catch up with friends or family, indulge in luxury food and drink and watch classic films on television. To celebrate in an eco-friendly way, imagine that the pressures of consumerism don't exist and you can give people presents that don't necessarily cost the earth. Break the cycle of rampant consumerism and throw-away goods: give eco-friendly presents instead. It might feel uncomfortable going against the grain, but if you don't break the cycle, who will?

Christmas generates around three million tonnes of waste in the UK – enough to fill 120 million wheelie bins. That includes one million Christmas cards and 83 square kilometres of wrapping paper – enough paper to wrap up Guernsey! Re-use old Christmas cards to make gift tags: cut the picture out in a square or circle, punch a hole in it and tie some string or ribbon through. Save good wrapping paper, gift tags, ribbons and string to use again. If you do buy new wrapping paper and ribbon, make sure it's biodegradable (avoid paper with a foil or plastic coating). Brown paper and raffia are understated, tasteful and entirely eco-friendly.

Don't spend silly money on presents: set up a 'Secret Santa'. Speak to your family or friends and agree on a price ceiling for presents: £10, £20 or £30 per person, depending on what everyone can afford. Write everyone's name on a piece of paper and put them in a hat. Everyone picks out a name and buys a present for that person. But don't give away who the present came from – it's a secret, remember!

Instead of cramming stockings with cheap plastic novelty toys that end up in the bin or charity shop, be inventive and fill them with things that connect people to the environment. Ideal eco-stocking fillers for adults and kids include:

- Organic satsumas
- Small bag of organic cashew nuts

- Pack of organic dates
- Notebook made from recycled paper
- Pair of walking socks
- Bar of Fairtrade chocolate
- Cinema voucher
- A year's subscription to *The Ecologist*
- Packet of tomato or sunflower seeds
- Refillable pen or pencil
- Refillable watercolour paint box
- Second-hand book
- Bird seed
- Wildflower seeds for the garden
- Calendar from Oxfam
- Toy from a charity shop
- Virtual gift – write a promise to do one thing for someone instead of a material present (a day's worth of gardening or a top-to-bottom house clean)
- A colourful 'bag for life'
- Little book on wildlife
- Adopt a turtle (www.mcsuk.org).

Whether for Christmas, birthdays, weddings, the birth of a baby or just because you want to give something to someone, choose eco-friendly presents:

- Dedicate a tree to someone you love. The Woodland Trust (www.wt-store.com) has planted more than eight million trees, creating new woodland throughout the UK. Trees are native to the UK and the recipient of the present receives a certificate with a personalised message and a map of the wood where the tree will be planted.

- Greenpeace (www.greenpeace.org) campaigns tirelessly, often in dangerous situations (imagine what it must be like on the Greenpeace boat, *Rainbow Warrior*, chasing determined Japanese whalers). Buy your best eco-buddy an annual subscription to Greenpeace for their birthday or Christmas.

- Buy UK-grown flowers, because they're not transported across the world or grown in developing countries with serious drought problems. Look for a Union Jack on the packaging. To make bunches of flowers look bigger and lusher, include some greenery from your garden, such as sprigs from evergreen plants that will last for a while in a vase. For very special occasions, order a bouquet of seasonal flowers grown in the UK from Wiggly Wigglers (www.wigglywigglers.com).

- Fairtrade fortnight (usually in February) often falls around St Valentine's Day, which is an excellent opportunity for promoting Fairtrade in your university. Set up a 'Fairtrade Sweet Shop' so students can buy their lovely chocolates. Or better still, organise a campus St Valentine's Day delivery service, in which volunteer organisers post chocolates to the object of your desire in the university internal post, with a Valentine message attached. For large orders of Fairtrade chocolate and other products see the Premcrest website (www.premcrest.co.uk).

- Icebreaker thermal underwear may not be everyone's idea of sexiness but it is stylish, certainly keeps the cold out and it's sustainably-sourced. UK suppliers of Icebreaker clothing include www.tauntonleisure.com and www.themountainfactor.com.

LIGHT GREEN Give at least one person an eco-gift next Christmas or birthday.

DEEP GREEN Buy Christmas stocking fillers, such as books, calendars, Fairtrade chocolate and Christmas cards from charity shops or not-for-profit organisations, instead of the supermarket.

TOP TIP Instead of buying a Christmas stocking, use one of your pillowcases.

Christmas cards

Some people like to receive Christmas emails or e-cards but others prefer to get a real card in the post. Emails use much less energy and natural resources but they can't be displayed on a shelf, so you don't get that Christmassy effect. As a compromise, send emails to your techie friends and real cards to non-techie friends and family.

Christmas trees

About six million Christmas trees are grown and sold in the UK each year, of which only about 10% are recycled. You probably won't have a tree at university but if you go home for the holidays, remind your family to recycle theirs. Your local council will have details of its tree recycling scheme.

Buy a Christmas tree grown in the UK, which has a lower carbon footprint that those transported from the US or Nordic countries. The British Christmas Tree Growers Association (www.christmastree.org.uk) is the trade association for those who grow Christmas trees in Great Britain and Northern Ireland. When you buy a tree, look out for the BCTGA logo – a Union Jack and a Christmas tree. Some people prefer to buy potted Christmas trees, which you can keep outside for most of the year and wheel in at Christmas: a good idea if you have a garden and can keep the tree watered.

Forget the brittle baubles made in China and go for something classier: make your Christmas tree more eco-friendly with natural decorations, which can be eaten, composted or recycled when you're bored with them. Here are some ideas for colour-themed decorations:

- Brown and orange:
  - Collect some pine cones when you go for a walk
  - Make some gingerbread men to hang on the tree
  - Buy some cinnamon sticks and tie them into little bundles
- Red:
  - String cranberries together to make red garlands to adorn your tree (you can get packs of these in the supermarkets from November onwards). Don't use holly berries – the birds need them for food during the winter.
- White and glittery
  - Cut shapes of angels or snowflakes from white paper
  - Cook popcorn and string it together to make pop-tinsel for your tree
  - Buy Fairtrade chocolates (in wrappers) and hang on the tree
  - Drape your tree in LED lights which last for years and use 80% less energy than standard fairy lights.

LIGHT GREEN Buy wrapping paper and cards made from FSC and/or recycled paper.

DEEP GREEN Buy a Christmas tree that has been grown in the UK.

New Year resolutions

Make a New Year resolution to give something back to the environment. Even if it's one small thing – like, 'I will buy eco-friendly washing up liquid from now on' – the environment will thank you. Dare your friends or family to make a New Year eco-resolution with you!

STAYING IN IS THE NEW GOING OUT

Going out every night is *de rigeur* for most students but eating out, going to the pub and clubbing is also a very quick way to use up all your money. How much money would you save if you stayed in one night a week with friends or housemates? Better still, how much more might you enjoy yourself? Laughter is good for your health, promoting neurological changes that reduce the secretion of stress hormones and strengthen the immune system. A single hour of laughter can have a positive physical effect on the body for up to 24 hours. What makes you laugh? How about:

- Pictionary: an active game in which one player has two minutes to draw a picture while the rest guess what it is – sounds simple but leads to rip-roaring laughter.
- Trivial Pursuit: test your brain cells against your opponents'.

- Charades: mime the most obscure films you can think of and stump your friends.

- Films: no need to go to the cinema and endure the rustling of other people's snack food. Get a DVD, invite some people round, make your own popcorn, crack open a beer and sit comfortably.

- Barbecue: if you have a garden, invite some friends round to spend a summer evening watching the sun set. You can get cheap barbecues from most DIY shops. Try to avoid buying disposable ones; even though they're made from aluminium, they get too dirty to recycle. Use FSC charcoal and cook organic or sustainably-sourced meat, fish or vegetables.

- Don't forget the classics – cards, backgammon and Scrabble™: cheap, eco-friendly entertainment that you can take travelling, for when you get bored with your iPod®.

SPORT, EXERCISE AND FUN

At the weekend or after a very long lecture, unwind in the park with friends with a game of Frisbee, football or rounders. You could consider joining your university's sport clubs if you want to participate regularly.

If you don't have a football, buy a Fairtrade football from Natural Collection (www.naturalcollection.com), which won't have been produced in a sweatshop or by child labourers. Perhaps your university would agree to stock Fairtrade footballs if you asked them (or asked the SU to speak on your behalf).

Walking is good exercise: your university may well have extensive grounds or be near parks or woodland. Take a picnic, a flask of tea, your camera and your best buddy and head off for a walk. Most councils provide information and maps for country and city walks.

Festivals

Get yer wellies on for Glastonbury, Reading, V Festival Leeds, T in the Park, Download, Isle of Wight, Creamfields, Beach Break Live and all the other brilliant festivals you'll be going to this year. The eco-friendliness of a festival is mainly the responsibility of the organisers but there are some things you can do to keep your eco-footprint small: keep an eye on your rubbish – recycle it or bin it but don't drop it; loose litter can harm wildlife. Take your stuff home with you: don't leave it behind in the hope that someone else will remove it – they probably won't. Take a reusable bottle, so you don't have to buy bottled water, and a bag for life so you can avoid collecting plastic bags as you buy your festival trinkets.

University events

Whether it's a Freshers' Fair, a Fairtrade taster event, a concert or an annual ball, try to persuade the organisers to make the event as eco-friendly as possible. Ask the university's Environment Officer to help you plan a zero waste event (you'll probably need volunteers to help) or the Purchasing Department to provide guidelines for suppliers on issues such as taking their waste away and disposing of it responsibly (for example, taking back packaging and the wooden pallets used to deliver goods).

Eco-friendliness might include: not using plastic cutlery, plates or glasses, supplying tap water in jugs, composting leftover food, purchasing the food and drink locally, buying organic produce, serving Fairtrade tea and coffee and stocking loos with recycled toilet paper. If all this gets done, the Vice-Chancellor (or whoever is hosting the event) will probably be delighted to announce that the university has done everything possible to ensure the event is sustainable!

If you want to campaign for your university to run eco-friendly events, ask the SU to look into the new guidelines for sustainable event management. The British Standard for Sustainable Event Management (BS8901) website (www.bs8901register.co.uk) has names of suppliers with a proven track record of good environmental performance and management.

SHOPPING LIST

Online eco-supermarkets
   www.ethicalsuperstore.com
   www.ecotopia.co.uk
   www.ecoretailonline.com

Lifestyle presents
   www.greenshop.co.uk
   www.biomelifestyle.com
   www.onevillage.com
   www.biggreenshop.co.uk

Outdoor wear and camping
   www.icebreaker.com
   www.tauntonleisure.com
   www.themountainfactor.com

Fashion
   www.americanapparel.co.uk
   www.peopletree.co.uk

www.thenaturalstore.co.uk
www.naturalcollection.com

Solar gadgets
www.solarkitsdirect.co.uk

Tree planting
www.wt-store.com

Fairtrade food and drink
www.premcrest.co.uk

Gardening, bird food, flower bouquets
www.wigglywigglers.com

Christmas
www.christmastree.org.uk

Wildlife conservation
www.mcsuk.org/marineworld/adopt-a-turtle/turtle +
adoption

Paint
www.ecosorganicpaints.com
www.greenshop.co.uk

Compost bins
www.recyclenow.com

Free stuff
   www.freecycle.org

Cosmetics, lotions and potions
   www.kingfishertoothpaste.com
   www.drhauschka.co.uk
   www.nealsyardremedies.com
   www.aubreyorganics.co.uk
   www.weleda.co.uk
   www.aveda.co.uk
   www.naturisimo.com
   www.naturalcollection.com
   www.greenpeople.co.uk
   www.essential-care.co.uk

TEMPLATES

The templates are for students who want to encourage their university to develop policies, or who want to write to organisations about their environmental practices:

ENVIRONMENTAL/SUSTAINABILITY POLICIES

Energy

The University of [name] Energy Policy is to reduce its buildings' and processes' carbon dioxide emissions in line with UK government carbon dioxide emissions reduction targets.

Greenhouse gases

The University of [name] Greenhouse Gases Policy is to reduce the emission of greenhouse gases (GHG) deriving from energy consumption and other activities that contribute to global warming. The GHG reduction targets include carbon dioxide, methane and volatile organic compounds, which have a significantly higher global warming potential than carbon dioxide.

Water

The University of [name] Water Policy is to review opportunities and implement measures for reducing the use of mains water and to reduce pollution entering its watercourses via stormwater (surface water) drains and sewers.

Sustainable buildings

The University of [name] Sustainable Buildings Policy is to build environmentally sustainable buildings to BREEAM 'Excellent' Standard and embed sustainable building best practice into the management of the University Estate. The University will ensure that any new buildings, or refurbished buildings, are planned, constructed and used to ensure the greatest energy and water efficiency and lowest carbon dioxide emissions. The University is committed to making full use of its existing buildings and, wherever possible when expansion is necessary, to the development of sites within walking or cycling distance of the remainder of the University.

Travel

The University of [name] is committed to sustainable travel, to encourage the use of efficient public and communal transport, bicycles and walking and to reduce carbon dioxide emissions from work-related travel and University-owned vehicles. The University discourages unnecessary travel and use of private motor transport for both travel to the University and travel for other work purposes during the day, with the aim of reducing traffic and parking in the city centre.

Waste

The University of [name] Waste Policy is to review opportunities and implement measures to minimise all types of waste generated by the University that is sent to landfill and increase the proportion of waste that is recycled.

Sustainable purchasing

The University of [name] Sustainable Purchasing Policy is to purchase products and services that reduce the University's environmental impacts locally and globally and minimise direct or indirect pollution to land, air and water. The University will work to ensure that the Sustainable Purchasing Policy is applied on a University-wide basis, to increase the use of sustainable products and products that can be recycled after use.

Biodiversity

The University of [name] Biodiversity Policy is to enhance the wildlife habitats in non-urban and urban environments owned by or related to the University and reduce the University's environmental impacts on biodiversity both locally and globally. The University will achieve this through a detailed Biodiversity Action Plan and implementation programme.

THE PROBLEM OF BEE DECLINE AND POLLINATION

Dear Prime Minister

Bee Colony Collapse Disorder, food supplies and the economy

I am very concerned about the current levels of research the UK is conducting into the causes of Bee Colony Collapse Disorder.

While the UK farming research budget may be limited, urgent research is needed to ensure that the UK can protect its bee populations and thereby guarantee sufficient crop pollination and food yields, so that our economy is not put at risk from potential food shortages. As the UK fruit economy is worth £165 million a year, a serious decline in the bee population could have a potentially disastrous impact on the farming community, the economy, food availability and costs.

Food self-sufficiency is likely to become increasingly important in the UK, as the country will probably need to grow more of its own food, due to changing global climatic and economic factors, such as failing food crops in the rest of the world due to climate change (flooding or drought) and rising food prices as a result of energy and transportation costs.

Colony Collapse Disorder is already devastating bee populations in the US, the EU and the UK. I urge you to consider putting more funds into research so that the National Bee Unit and the British Beekeepers' Association can increase their research output.

Yours sincerely,
[Name]
[University]

PERSUADING YOUR UNIVERSITY TO BE MORE ECO-FRIENDLY

Dear Vice-Chancellor

Environmental improvements in the university

Students in the University are increasingly concerned about whether the University is doing enough to reduce its environmental footprint. For example, it has been noticed that much of the printer paper used in the University is not from recycled or sustainably-managed sources and that recycling facilities are not available in all departments.

As you are probably aware, environmental issues are high on the government agenda and environmental improvement is key to the University's reputation, in the eyes of students, visitors and the Higher Education Funding Council for England (HEFCE). The HEFCE Estates Management Statistics recently added extra environmental criteria to its annual reporting criteria. The HEFCE EMS is one of the vehicles the government can use to put pressure on universities to reduce energy and waste, use water more efficiently and procure sustainably-sourced goods and services. These environmental measures are necessary in order to slow the pace of global warming and the fast decline of the world's natural resources.

To establish the current position of the University with regard to reducing its environmental footprint, I am enquiring whether the University is able to provide me with any of the following documentation:

- University Environmental/Sustainability Policy
- University Environmental/Sustainability Targets
- University Energy Strategy
- University Waste Strategy
- University Water Strategy
- University Biodiversity Strategy
- University Travel Plan/Strategy
- University Greenhouse Gases Strategy
- University Sustainable Buildings Strategy
- University Sustainable Purchasing Strategy

I can be contacted at the following [Postal address] [email address]

Yours sincerely,
[Name]

PETROCHEMICALS IN COSMETICS AND CLEANING PRODUCTS

Dear [Name of Company/Sir or Madam]

Phasing out petrochemical ingredients

I am writing to raise my concern at the continuing use of petrochemicals in your cleansing products. While many companies are starting to use (certified) natural ingredients in their products, I have not encountered any information on your website that implies your company has a strategy for phasing out potentially harmful chemicals that are currently used in your products.

As consumer demand is critical to the success of your business, perhaps your business would benefit from paying more attention to leading scientists from around the world who are increasingly concerned about the build-up of chemical pollution in water. Evidence shows that petrochemicals are already found in the bodies of most human beings and wildlife and that this can affect their organs and immune systems, with potentially fatal consequences.

Petrochemicals are absorbed through the skin and research on animals indicates these chemicals can cause harm to vital organs. It is likely that in the near future, conclusive scientific evidence will show that petrochemicals are harmful to humans. As this evidence emerges and becomes widely publicised in the media, your customer base is likely to decline, as they switch to less harmful products.

Examples of customers quickly switching to environmentally-responsible products include the use of cloth bags instead of plastic bags, Ecover detergents, Fairtrade bananas and free-range eggs. Sainsbury, M&S, Unilever and other big businesses are starting to see the economic benefits of meeting customer demand for 'green' products.

I would like to know how your company plans to improve its corporate responsibility – specifically with regard to reducing petrochemical use in your products, in order to reduce pollution and the potential risk to human and marine animal health.

If you would kindly send me any of the following documents I would be most grateful:

- Company Corporate Responsibility Policy
- Company Environmental/Sustainability Policy
- Company Environmental/Sustainability Targets

Yours sincerely,
[Name]
[University]

LOBBYING AGAINST GM FOOD

Dear (name of supermarket Chief Executive)

Dear (name of Minister for the Environment)

I am very concerned at the prospect of having no choice but to consume food that contains GM ingredients. There is no conclusive evidence that GM is safe for humans or the environment and it is worrying that the UK government seems to be determined to introduce GM crops to the UK, regardless of the fact that the majority of UK citizens do not want to eat GM food. The Greenpeace Contamination Register Report (published February 2008) reports the following:

- Contamination incidents (as of 2007): 39
- Total number of contamination incidents: 216
- Cases of illegal release of GMOs in 2007: 11
- Cases of illegal sales of GM zebra danio fish: 4
- Spillage of GM seed from trucks in Japan and Brazil: 2
- Illegal growing of GM maize in Mexico and Peru
- Contamination and illegal release of GM cotton, fish, maize, oilseed rape, papaya, rice and soybean
- Herbicide tolerant rice was released into the environment illegally, causing big problems in the rice industry

Evidence on growing GM crops suggests that:

- GM crops require more herbicide to be used in the long term than non-GM crops (resulting in an increase in chemical pollution).

- GM has not produced successful pest-resistant crops and some pests thrive on GM more than on non-GM crops.

- GM crops can harm beneficial insects, for example bees, which are crucial for pollination and therefore crop yields.

- GM crops require increased use of agri-chemicals and lead to a decrease in wildlife on farms (for example, oilseed rape and sugar beet).

- GM contamination of wild flowers in the UK has already occurred and there is evidence of many cases of GM contamination world-wide.

- GM creates superweeds that are resistant to several herbicides.

- Chemicals used on GM crops require large amounts of fossil fuels which contribute directly to global warming and climate change.

- Scientific evidence is emerging that GM can damage the internal organs and immune systems of experimental animals fed on GM crops and that humans can also be harmed by the effects of breathing in GM pollen.

- GM farming gradually degrades the soil, leading to a decrease in essential minerals necessary for human health. Also, soil desertification is a growing problem in the UK and the rest of the world, at a time when food production is more important than ever before.

Billons of pounds of tax-payers' money are spent evaluating the risks of GM crops. It seems that GM production and the associated risk is something that most UK citizens do not want, nor do they want to eat GM food or food accidentally contaminated with GM ingredients.

I therefore urge you firmly to refuse to allow GM products to be sold in the UK.

Yours sincerely,
[Name]
[University]

FURTHER READING

Before you rush out to the shops, check whether any of these titles are available second-hand (for example on Amazon, www.amazon.co.uk).

Antczak, Stephen & Gina *Cosmetics Unmasked*, Harper Collins, London, 2001

Barclay, Liz *Green Living for Dummies*, John Wiley & Sons Ltd, 2007

Christensen, Karen *Eco Living; A Handbook for the Twenty-first Century*, Piatkus, 2000

Hickman, Leo *A Life Stripped Bare; Tiptoeing Through the Ethical Minefield*, Eden Project Books, 2005

Poyzer, Penny *No Waste Like Home*, Virgin Books Ltd, 2005

Royte, Elizabeth *Bottlemania: How Water Went on Sale and Why We Bought It*, Bloomsbury, 2008

Salter-Green, Elizabeth *The Toxic Consumer*, Impact Publishing, 2007

Scott, Nicky *Reduce, Reuse, Recycle: An Easy Household Guide*, Green Books, 2004

Deep Economy
Economics as if the World Mattered
Bill McKibben

The bestselling author of *The End of Nature* issues an impassioned call to arms for an economy that enriches communities and enables our lives.

"An important and multifaceted book."
- **Lord Robert May of Oxford,** former President of the Royal Society

"A timely warning that infinite economic growth is impossible on a finite planet... A new smart form of economics." **- Dr Derek Wall,** Green Party of England and Wales

9781851685967 - HB - £16.99
9781851685769 - PB - £9.99

The Blue Death
Disease, Disaster and the Water We Drink
Robert D. Morris

From devastating outbreaks of cholera and cryptosporidium to potentially carcinogenic water treatments and the threat of bioterrorism, public health expert Robert Morris criss-crosses the globe to provide a riveting account of the dangers lurking in the water we drink.

"Engrossing and disquieting" - *Publishers Weekly*

9781851685752 - HB - £16.99

Oilopoly
Putin, Power and the Rise of the New Russia
Marshall Goldman

This deft, informative narrative chronicles Russia's meteoric return to the world stage as an oil Superpower. Marshall Goldman recounts this with panache, as only one of the world's leading authorities on Russia could.

"A gripping, highly topical, and important book - and what a rattling good read!"
- Richard Sakwa, Associate Fellow of the Russia and Eurasia Programme at the Royal Institute of International Affairs

9781851686216 - HB - £18.99
9781851686469 - PB - £10.99

The Secret War With Iran
The 30-Year Covert Struggle for Control of a "Rogue State"
Ronen Bergman

Ronen Bergman, one of Israel's top investigative reporters, exposes the attempts of CIA, Mossad and their European counterparts to control Iran, dubbed by some observers as one of the most formidable sponsors of terror in the world today. Riveting and urgent.

"Thoroughly researched and persuasively argued, Bergman's brief against Iran adds a powerful voice to a contentious debate."
- Publishers Weekly

9781851686223 - HB - £16.99
9781851686766 - PB - £9.99